Portraits of
Shakespeare

Portraits of
Shakespeare

KATHERINE DUNCAN-JONES

Bodleian Library
UNIVERSITY OF OXFORD

First published in 2015 by the Bodleian Library
Broad Street
Oxford OX1 3BG

www.bodleianshop.co.uk

ISBN 978 1 85124 405 8

Text © Katherine Duncan-Jones, 2015
Images, unless specified on page 121,
© Bodleian Library, University of Oxford, 2015

Cover design by Dot Little at the Bodleian Library
Text designed and typeset in 11½ on 15 Van Dijck
by illuminati, Grosmont
Printed and bound by Prosperous Printing Co. Ltd, China
on FSC® certified 157 gsm Neo Matt

British Library Catalogue in Publishing Data
A CIP record of this publication is available from the British Library

Contents

Prologue

HERE ARE THREE IMAGES of William Shakespeare that were tacitly acknowledged as authentic likenesses by people who had been familiar with his appearance. These are the Stratford bust (a memorial erected in Holy Trinity Church, Stratford-upon-Avon, about seven years after his death); the so-called 'Droeshout engraving', which appears on the title page of the 1623 First Folio edition of his works; and the painting known as the 'Chandos portrait', painted in oil on canvas and dating from about 1610.

All three portraits are unsatisfactory for a variety of reasons, which will be explored in the following pages. The Stratford bust is vacuous and stiff, while the Droeshout engraving is primitive and ill-proportioned. These two have suffered excessive interference in the name of restoration. In both cases these interventions prevent us from gaining a fully reliable sense of their original appearance. The Chandos portrait, though fresh and animated, seems to be a rapidly painted oil sketch rather than a fully finished portrait created by a skilled professional limner. In later times, from the early eighteenth century onwards, the unsatisfactory nature of all three images has appeared to leave the field open for the discovery – or, failing that, the manufacture – of previously unrecognized images that Shakespeare's many admirers might find more pleasing.

There is reason to suspect that some admirers of Shakespeare's writing were keen to obtain likenesses of the poet as early as 1599/1600. But did such a likeness ever exist? Given the unbroken continuity of Shakespeare's fame, one would expect that a really good image taken from life, if such an image existed, would have been identified as such in an inscription, perhaps including the sitter's birth-date and/or age, or his coat of arms and motto. A plausible time for such a painting to be commissioned by Shakespeare himself would be in or soon after 1596/7, when he acquired the right to display a coat of arms that affirmed his status as a gentleman. But no such portrait appears to have survived. If it did exist, in the light of the fame of Shakespeare and his plays, it would have been much copied. A family in possession of such a picture would surely be proud of it, transmitting that pride to their descendants. Since his lifetime there has never been a prolonged period during which some, if not all, of Shakespeare's works have not been both admired and closely studied. This should have ensured that an original portrait, or early copy of one, would have been cherished. Even during the English Civil War and Commonwealth period – with the ban on public performances of plays from 1642 to 1662 – the publication of the 1623 First Folio, followed by that of the Second Folio in 1632, ensured that some people in possession of good libraries could at least read Shakespeare's plays. Provided they were not Puritans, families who lived in noble households could even perform them in private.

In addition to playgoers and lovers of Shakespeare's verse, there is a third category of people who may be assumed to have cherished original images of Shakespeare, if they existed: his close family and friends in and around Stratford-upon-Avon. Few individual chattels are mentioned in Shakespeare's will, apart from the 'broad silver and gilt bowl' explicitly bequeathed to his elder daughter, Susanna; the poet's sword, bequeathed to his young friend Thomas Combe; and that notorious and never-to-be-forgotten 'second-best bed' bequeathed to the wife who was shortly to become a widow. It is plausible that Mistress Susanna Hall would have inherited a portrait of her father. If so, it has left no trace in surviving records. We have two texts of Shakespeare's will, but no copy of the inventory of chattels that was likely to have been made either before or after his death, in which both pictures and books would have figured. Shakespeare's less loved younger daughter Judith might also have wanted such a memento. Judging by the will, Judith had enraged her dying father by marrying the unreliable wine-seller Thomas Quiney, who was not a good match, either financially or morally. He had made another Stratford girl pregnant while preparing to marry Judith Shakespeare. Even so, the Quineys' first son, born a few months after the death of his celebrated grandfather, was christened Shakespeare, and the Quiney family might have cherished a visual image of their illustrious forebear.

Some of Shakespeare's more prosperous Stratford friends, such as Thomas Combe and Thomas Russell, would probably have liked to possess an image of Shakespeare, yet no evidence survives of any such portrait being preserved in a house in Stratford or its environs. To me this strongly suggests that none existed. But for many after-comers, this absence has left the field wide open. From the late nineteenth century until now, many so-called discoveries have been made. Indeed, Dr Tarnya Cooper, curator of sixteenth-century portraits at the National Portrait Gallery, has remarked that 'Every five to 10 years, a "new" Shakespeare portrait will appear … There are between 50 and 100 images in the National Portrait Gallery stacks that were at one time considered to be him.'[1]

Determination to discover a reliable likeness of Shakespeare – an issue of long-standing fascination – is if anything on the increase.

Again and again, the three earliest surviving images of the great poet-playwright have been viewed as artistically disappointing and frustratingly unrevealing in terms of the playwright's real-life appearance, and have left his admirers hungry for something better. They have also prompted recurring questions. Can we be certain that none of the surviving images of Shakespeare originates within his lifetime? Do the author portraits made of his contemporaries, such as Ben Jonson, shed any light on this mysterious absence? Are there any useful clues to be found in places other than Stratford, such as Oxford and London? And can these three portraits, together with the many imitations, commemorative effigies and memorials, tell us anything at all about Shakespeare's life?

ANNO DÑI   ÆTATIS SVÆ 21
1585.

QVOD ME NVTRIT
ME DESTRVIT

ONE

Shakespeare and the 'author portrait'

OWADAYS WE ARE apt to take it for granted that we can see what writers look like or, in the case of dead writers, what they looked like. New novels generally include an author photograph on the back or front flap, and so do many non-fiction books. In truth, except for writers of memoirs or autobiographies, there is often no necessary or relevant connection between a writer's physical appearance and their particular skills and preoccupations, or the power of their writing style. But the desire for a visual image is widespread.

It has been stated rather firmly that with Shakespeare, portraiture 'does not matter. Nor should we be concerned with the accuracy of the Chandos portrait in the National Gallery or the veracity of the engraving in the First Folio. Shakespeare was a genius, not a personality.'[1]

Nevertheless, desire to see an image of a much admired writer – in this instance, Shakespeare – is both widespread and compelling, and is nothing new. As long ago as 1824 James Boaden described this longing: 'A reader who rises from the perusal of Shakespeare's writings will be apt, from a fanciful analogy, to invest his person with extraordinary graces; and his portrait is required to reflect all the intelligence of his works.'[2] Popular demand for an image of Shakespeare has, if anything, increased in the last few decades.

1 (*previous spread*) Portrait supposedly of Christopher Marlowe, dated 1585.

Passions may be powerfully aroused over the issue of a dead writer's physical appearance. Heated debates about the authenticity or otherwise of two portraits thought by some to be of Jane Austen provide a case in point. This particular debate has been fuelled by deeply held convictions that the images in question do, or do not, conform to what Jane Austen *ought* to look like, according to the most devoted 'Janeites'.

Similarly, there was great delight when, in 1953, a late Elizabethan portrait was discovered among a pile of discarded rubbish outside Corpus Christi College, Cambridge, the college where Christopher Marlowe had been a scholar (FIG. 1). Though 1585, the date included in the painting, is compatible with this being a portrait of Marlowe, there is no sound evidence that its subject truly is Marlowe, rather than some other alumnus of Corpus Christi – or even an unidentified young gentleman unconnected to the college. It seems odd, in any case, that such a portrait turned up in or near Corpus Christi. One would not expect a college to possess a portrait of one of its alumni unless this individual were remarkably distinguished or a wealthy benefactor.

It is also hard to reconstruct circumstances in which Marlowe – an impoverished student – and already extremely elusive in his movements, with frequent absences from his college – might have sat for this portrait. Nor can we imagine who would have paid for such an artefact or guess why, if it belonged to Corpus, it was so nearly thrown away. Yet the excitement of Marlovians about this discovery has never died down. It is rare for a biography of Marlowe or an edition of his plays or poems not to include a reproduction of the painting.

It shouldn't really matter whether a writer's appearance tallies with preconceptions aroused by study of their literary works, yet somehow, for many readers and admirers, it seems that it does. Again and again, the earliest surviving images of Shakespeare have been viewed as artistically disappointing and frustratingly unrevealing in terms of the playwright's real-life appearance, and have left his admirers hungry for something better.

Images of playwrights pose particular problems. Most plays, whether written in the sixteenth century or today, incorporate a wide variety of voices and characters, none of which should be regarded as direct reflections of the writer's own personality or appearance. In the early 1590s many audiences, and some readers, were familiar with Shakespeare's plays, but they did not necessarily know that he was their author. The earliest plays to be printed with his name on the title page did not appear until 1598, probably a decade after they were written. In contrast to today, plays in the late Elizabethan period were regularly both collaboratively and hastily written. Collaborative authorship was a common practice, as is being increasingly demonstrated with reference to those of Shakespeare's plays written either early, as were the three *Henry VI* plays, or late, as was *Henry VIII*. This is one of the reasons why audience curiosity about the specific identity of a playwright was not widespread. Plays were advertised by subject matter rather than by author. The title pages of printed plays often included a summary of the highlights of the play in question, but rarely identified the play's author or authors. The general idea that the pleasure of reading a play-text might be somehow enhanced by seeing an image of its writer was apparently not yet established.

In fact, it was as a lyrical, erotic and highly rhetorical non-dramatic poet that Shakespeare's name and fame were first securely recorded and celebrated. His two narrative poems, *Venus and Adonis* (1593) and *The Rape of Lucrece* (1594), were immediate best-sellers, being widely quoted, admired, parodied and imitated, especially by young readers. Both are prefaced by epistles to Shakespeare's then patron, Henry Wriothesley, signed off by 'William Shakespeare'. It is not surprising, therefore, that it is thanks to his fame as a non-dramatic poet that Shakespeare is first recorded with reference to an author portrait.

The following testimony suggests that a portrait of Shakespeare may have been in existence as early as the late sixteenth century, when the writer's fame and popularity reached their first peak. A character in a late-Elizabethan Cambridge play expresses his intense admiration for Shakespeare thus: 'O Sweet Master Shakespeare, I'll have his picture in my study at the court.'[3]

The play in which this line is spoken, entitled *The First Part of the Return from Parnassus*, concerns the problems encountered by Cambridge alumni when they leave the university (Parnassus) and try to secure gainful employment. The play seems to have been both written and performed at St John's College during the Christmas vacation of 1599/1600.[4] The line quoted above, delivered by a wealthy but rather dim-witted character called Gullio, who wants to pass off some of Shakespeare's verses as his own, testifies both to the tremendous popularity of Shakespeare and his writings by this date, and to the possible existence and availability of some kind of author portrait that may have been in demand among Shakespeare's younger fans – rather like a student poster of a favourite pop singer in modern times. Shakespeare's non-dramatic verse and, especially, his elegant and amorous long narrative poem *Venus and Adonis* are greatly relished by the foolish gallant Gullio – so much so that he plans to pass off passages from Shakespeare's verse as his own composition. If an image of Shakespeare truly existed around 1600, then, it is quite likely to have been associated with his narrative poems rather than with his plays.

Gullio's desire to 'have his [Shakespeare's] picture' for his own personal perusal may, therefore, testify to the beginning of some interest in the poet's appearance. His 'real' appearance – albeit in stage costume – may already have been familiar to some young men because of his performances on stage as an actor. Young gallants such as Gullio formed a major and lively segment of playhouse audiences. However, there is little other reason to believe that playgoers took much interest in possessing images of leading actors other than fools and clowns.

If a picture of Shakespeare were truly in existence as early as 1600, it might not have been a particularly sophisticated likeness. Possibly it was so unlike later images of him that copies, if any survive, have not been identified as such in modern times. Possibly, too, since we have sound evidence that Shakespeare's friend and colleague the actor Richard Burbage was a skilled painter as well as a brilliant performer, Burbage portrayed Shakespeare in an image that has either disappeared entirely, or survives only in a version no longer recognized as deriving from a Burbage original. There is further exploration of Burbage's connection to the story of Shakespeare's portraits in Chapter 4.

Engraved title-page portraits of English poets began to appear quite frequently during the 1590s, but generally they fronted more substantial, or more elite, writings than play-books. It was not until 1598 that Shakespeare's name began to appear on the title page of printed texts of his plays. Some of these texts were later labelled as Bad Quartos by scholars, and many are undoubtedly clumsily printed. In contrast, *Venus and Adonis* and *Lucrece* were both elegantly and accurately printed and formatted (FIG. 2). Though Shakespeare's name does not occur on their title pages, it does appear once one turns the page. Both volumes include dedicatory epistles addressed by Shakespeare to his young patron, Henry Wriothesley, 3rd earl of Southampton, on the second leaf, and the sign-offs to these epistles draw attention to the poet's identity: 'Your honour's in all duty / William Shakespeare' (*Venus and Adonis*) and 'your lordship's in all duty / William Shakespeare' (*Lucrece*). Shakespeare's authorship of his *Sonnets* in 1609 is more

2 Title page of Shakespeare's narrative poem *Venus and Adonis* (1593). From a unique copy of the first edition from the Bodleian Library, Arch. G e.31(2).

emphatically attributed, with his name visible on every opening in the full title; 'Shake-speares Sonnets' is repeated at the top of every page. There is no engraving or woodcut frontispiece depicting the poet in any of these volumes. This is not particularly mysterious or surprising, as becomes apparent if we examine the longer tradition of author portraits.

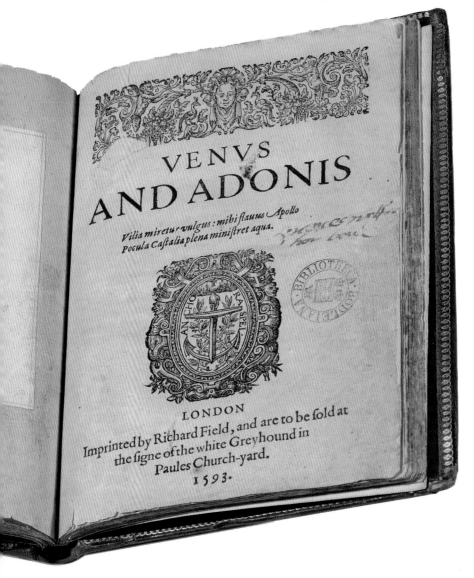

VENVS AND ADONIS

Vilia miretur vulgus: mihi flauus Apollo
Pocula Castalia plena ministret aqua.

LONDON
Imprinted by Richard Field, and are to be fold at
the figne of the white Greyhound in
Paules Church-yard.
1593.

Portraits in Oxford

The genre of the author portrait was well analysed by David Piper, who discussed its origins in late antiquity. As Piper said, the tradition may be seen as

> arising from the fact that the author is talking to you. The printed word is the spoken word materialized: if someone talks to you, you turn to the speaker to see who it is, and so when reading his words you turn equally naturally to the portrait frontispiece to see who is addressing you.[5]

Whether fashioned in late antiquity or in the Renaissance, the very earliest author portraits tend to be symbolic rather than naturalistic. Few appear to be speaking likenesses, and only rarely does the author portrayed appear to make eye contact with the viewer. We should survey this wide and long-established tradition before examining depictions of Shakespeare – especially so since images of this kind are exceptionally well represented within the Bodleian Library in Oxford, which at the time of its foundation in 1602 (about 150 years before the foundation of the British Museum) and for two centuries beyond was, in effect, England's national library. It was the country's most significant collection of literature, both in manuscript and in print.

Of all the possible locations for a portrait of Shakespeare, Oxford seems one of the most likely (the others being Stratford-upon-Avon and London; the latter is discussed further in Chapter 3). It was later home to the Bodleian Library, and was already a natural staging post on the journey from Shakespeare's home in Stratford to London, a journey which he must have made many times.

Many author portraits may be encountered within the Bodleian's great collections of illuminated manuscripts. More publicly accessible examples may be viewed on and around the physical fabric of the Bodleian Library itself. The most conspicuous one,

BEATI PACIFICI

RECNANTE D.IACOBO REGVM DOCTISSIMO
MVNIFICENTISSIMO OPTIMO HÆ MVSIS
EXTRVCTÆ MOLES.CONGESTA BIBLIOTHECA
ET QVÆCVNQVE ADHVC DEERANT AD SPLEN
DOREM ACADEMIÆ FELICITER TENTATA
COEPTA ABSOLVTA. SOLI DEO GLORIA.

3 James I and VI donating his works to the University of Oxford (on the viewer's right) and to Fame (on the viewer's left): sculptured scene by John Clark (1620) which appears on the Tower of the Five Orders in the Bodleian Quadrangle.

probably the first that will catch the eye of a new visitor to the Bodleian, is the grandiose sculptured scene on the fourth storey of the Tower of the Five Orders, above the Great Gate. This depicts King James I and VI donating his own literary works jointly to the University of Oxford, which is shown symbolically as a veiled woman, and to Fame, who blows her trumpet. It was constructed by the sculptor John Clark in 1620, and is based on the frontispiece to the king's Latin works published earlier that year (FIG. 3). Many more portraits are to be seen inside the Library. Indeed, the large U-shaped upper storey of Sir Thomas Bodley's building, now known as the Upper Reading Room, was previously known as the Gallery.

However, today's visitors are faced with a small but perplexing question. Why are there no early images of Shakespeare anywhere in Oxford, despite the fact that both the Bodleian Library and the colleges are, as a whole, extremely rich in author portraits?

The Upper Reading Room of the Bodleian is decorated with a long frieze depicting 202 'heads' that was painted directly onto the building's internal stonework – artwork which was originally carried out in 1619.[6] The original selection of heads for the frieze was determined by the distinctive preoccupations both of the Library's founder, Sir Thomas Bodley, who died in 1613, and of the first Bodley's Librarian, Thomas James, who retired from the post in 1620. No living writers were included (FIG. 4).

By 1619, when the frieze was painted, Shakespeare had been dead for three years. As a dead male poet of considerable fame he might appear to qualify for inclusion. However, it should come as no great surprise that he is not, in fact, included among the 202 men depicted. Had the frieze been planned a few years later, after the publication of the splendid First Folio of his plays in 1623, which was dedicated to the noble brothers William Herbert, earl of Pembroke, and Philip Herbert, earl of Montgomery – both of them strong favourites of the king – Shakespeare might have stood some chance of making it to the Bodleian's Hall of Fame. But he

4 Portraits of four writers from the frieze of the Bodleian Library's Upper Reading Room: the Greek playwright Sophocles, the Greek historian Thucydides, the late-eighteenth-century Italian writer Bartolomeo Platina and the early-sixteenth-century Italian poet Lodovico Ariosto.

would probably not have qualified. He was not a man of learning in any conventional or academic sense, nor were vernacular plays performed in public theatres generally viewed as texts worthy of the serious attention of scholars and academics. For one thing, in contrast to many humanist scholars, such as those depicted on the Bodleian's frieze, his reputation was largely confined to the British Isles. Even as a non-dramatic poet, both of whose long poems were derived from classical sources, Shakespeare would not have seemed to qualify for visually iconic status in Bodley's great Library. Thomas Bodley regarded play-books as quite unsuitable items for perusal in his Library. In the interests of what was then classified as 'learning', he also mostly excluded images of secular English writers from the painted frieze.

Only four playwrights are shown on the Bodleian frieze, two Greek, two Roman: Sophocles, Euripedes, Terence and Aristophanes. Among English writers who appear, the only one who is likely to be immediately recognized by most modern visitors is Geoffrey Chaucer.

According to the antiquary Thomas Hearne, who played a major role in identifying the subjects of the much faded frieze portraits in the 1720s, Bodley had intended his great library to serve 'chiefly for books against the Roman Catholics'.[7] This extraordinarily limited mission, perhaps slightly exaggerated by Hearne, helps to explain both the presence in the frieze of some extremely obscure individuals – such as Bodley's personal friends Thomas Sparkes and John Spenser – and the absence from it of many writers and men of learning whom a later age might regard as far more noteworthy, such as Thomas More, William Camden, William Shakespeare and Ben Jonson, to name but four.

However, despite Sir Thomas Bodley's stated preferences, the Bodleian soon evolved into a library celebrated for its magnificently wide embrace.

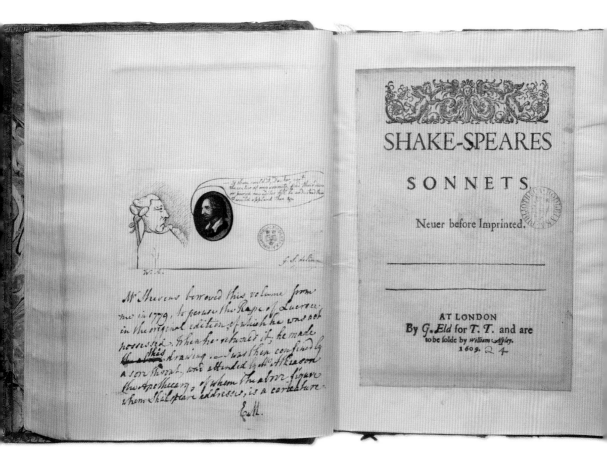

Many major benefactions contributed to its success, such as that of Robert Burton's library in 1650, and the posthumous one of Edmond Malone's collection of Shakespeare-related books and manuscripts in 1721. Among many other riches, the Malone collection includes a copy of *Shakespeare's Sonnets* (1609) to which George Steevens, a rival and rather malicious Shakespeare scholar, added a cut-out roundel portrait of Shakespeare, which he embellished further with a caricature of the apothecary who had recently treated Malone for an infection (FIG. 5).[8]

5 Drawings and writings by George Steevens and Edmond Malone on the page facing the title page in a copy of *Shakespeare's Sonnets* (1609). Bodleian Library, Arch. G d.41 (2).

Portraits of other writers

Portraits of poets on frontispieces, sometimes of great elaboration and sophistication, became fairly common in the later Elizabethan period. They presumably reflect burgeoning confidence in the value and marketability of contemporary English literature, leading also to growing interest in the specific character and appearance of writers. By tracing the evolution of the author portraits of five significant writers, it is possible to begin to understand more clearly why an author portrait of Shakespeare done from life is so elusive. Geoffrey Chaucer, Sir John Harington, Samuel Daniel, Michael Drayton and Ben Jonson all shed light on this question. If the origins and careers of these writers were in many respects strongly analogous to Shakespeare's, why were they so strikingly different with regard to portraiture?

Geoffrey Chaucer, Sir John Harington & Samuel Daniel

Until quite recently Geoffrey Chaucer held his own as the only writer other than Shakespeare studied by all schoolchildren in the UK. Works by Chaucer have also been included as part of the core curriculum in most university courses in English language and literature. He is also notable as the only medieval English poet whose image is immediately recognizable. Numerous paintings and drawings of Chaucer survive from the first two decades after his death in 1400. Broadly conforming to a type, these establish a very familiar image of 'Dan Chaucer' – a paunchy man, who wears a loose gown that falls just below the knees and a cap with a long scarf falling from it. He usually holds a rosary in his left hand, while with his right he either points to a text, or – more often – clutches an inkhorn. In either case, the right hand draws attention to Chaucer's status as a substantial and copious writer. There is a rather clumsy half-length version of the latter portrait

6 Oil on panel portrait of Geoffrey Chaucer. Bodleian Library LP 8.

Caucer 1400.

type, painted on panel in the late seventeenth century, in the
Bodleian Library (FIG. 6). Familiarity with Chaucer's image
became even more widely diffused as his works reached print,
both separately and collectively, and other matter was added to
supplement it, such as his coat of arms and family tree, as well as
various literary works not now believed to be authentic. Printed
portraiture of Chaucer reached a climax in 1598, with the inclusion of particularly splendid arms and a family tree flanking the
figure of the poet in the edition of Chaucer's writings prepared
by Thomas Speght. As his literary status rose, so did his (alleged)
social status. Several Elizabethan commentators declared him,
wrongly, to have been a knight.[9]

The case of Sir John Harington of Kelston (1560–1612) is very
different. Though almost exactly contemporary to Shakespeare
in lifespan, Harington was unlike him in virtually every other
respect. He was born into a wealthy and privileged family. His
godmother was Queen Elizabeth herself, and his godfather was
William Herbert, 2nd earl of Pembroke – father of the younger
William Herbert, who was to be the joint dedicatee of the First
Folio of Shakespeare's plays in 1623. Though Harington never held
any significant court office, the queen was particularly fond of him.
She wrote letters to him while he was a schoolboy at Eton, and
her special affection for him endured. She invited him to a private
audience with her in the Christmas season of 1602/3, only three
months before her death. At this last meeting she confessed to
Harington that she believed herself to be mortally ill – something
of which her other courtiers were as yet blithely unaware.

It was to his godmother the queen that Harington dedicated
his *magnum opus*, a complete verse translation of Lodovico Ariosto's
chivalric romance *Orlando Furioso*. This was printed in 1591 by the
Stratford-born printer Richard Field, who was to print and publish
Shakespeare's *Venus and Adonis* just two years later. Harington's

work was altogether a much grander and more substantial production than Shakespeare's, delivered with no false modesty on the
part of the translator. The poem's elaborately ornamented title
page (FIG. 7) incorporates a portrait of Harington himself, bottom
centre, which is a little more than twice the size of the portrait

of Lodovico Ariosto, of whose long chivalric poem Harington was the translator. In a characteristically playful touch, Harington has caused the engraver, Thomas Coxon, also to include, bottom right, an image of Harington's faithful spaniel Bungay, who is shown devotedly gazing at his master as he awaits his next command. The general message of the title page is that Harington is a distinctively brilliant writer who has the power to inspire both love and loyalty. He is loved by the queen herself, to whom the work is confidently dedicated.

Another of Shakespeare's contemporaries, Samuel Daniel (1562–1619), had particularly close links with the Bodleian.[10] Like Shakespeare, he wrote both plays and non-dramatic poetry. His double volume, composed of a collection of sonnets followed by a love complaint in stanzaic verse, was a definite influence on Shakespeare, whose *Sonnets*, succeeded by the poem 'A Lover's Complaint', echoed that structure. Shakespeare also drew on Daniel's *Civil Wars*, verse accounts of the Wars of the Roses, when composing the trilogy of plays now known as *Henry VI 1, 2* and *3*. Though he was by no means as well connected as John Harington, Daniel enjoyed origins and connections that were distinctly loftier than Shakespeare's. He was an alumnus of Magdalen Hall in Oxford, where he formed a strong friendship with the Italian scholar and translator John Florio, who introduced him both to the Italian language and to contemporary Italian poetry. Daniel received noble patronage during the reign of Elizabeth I, and in the early Jacobean era composed royal masques, especially for the queen, Anne of Denmark. Daniel was also quick off the mark in praising Sir Thomas Bodley and his newly enlarged Library, in a poem to be found only in the Bodleian's unique presentation copy of the 1601 edition of his *Works*.

In terms of visual prominence, the climax of Daniel's career occurred in 1609. His latest revision of the much revised *Civil Wars*

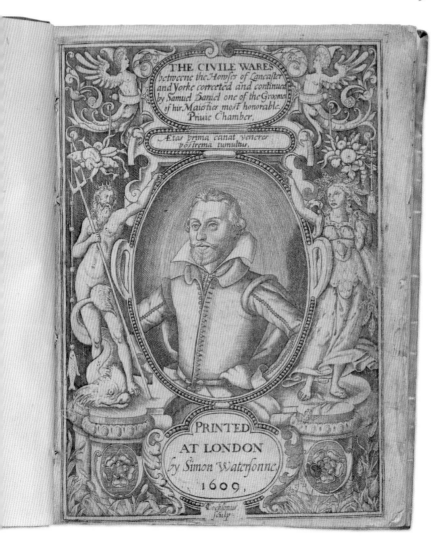

8 Portrait of Samuel Daniel on the title page of his historical narrative poem *Civil Wars* (engraved by Thomas Coxon 1609). Bodleian Library, 4° A 26 Art.BS.

was published that year with a frontispiece depicting the poet, half-length, engraved by Thomas Coxon (FIG. 8). He is flanked by symbolic figures of Neptune and Flora. Daniel was a groom of the chamber – that is, a minor servant of the monarch – and was not slow to proclaim his enjoyment of court favour in the early Jacobean period. Shakespeare, too, became a groom of the chamber when his playing company gained royal patronage from King James I, but he did not present himself as such visually to the reading public, as Daniel so emphatically did.

Michael Drayton and Ben Jonson

The lives, careers and social origins of both Michael Drayton (1563–1631) and Ben Jonson (1572–1637) are in many respects remarkably analogous to Shakespeare's. Michael Drayton's father was a Warwickshire tanner, making him comparable both in geographical region and social status to Shakespeare's father, a Warwickshire glover. Both were craftsmen who worked with animal skins, and both of their poet-sons were born in 1563. Jonson's stepfather was a master bricklayer, and for a while the future poet and playwright laboured at that trade. Drayton appears to have enjoyed a good education within a gentleman's household, while Jonson was Camden's scholar at Westminster School. Neither proceeded to a university. Early on in their careers, both Drayton and Jonson earned money, as Shakespeare did, by writing plays either collaboratively or independently for London playing companies. Drayton is most fully documented as doing so for The Lord Admiral's Men. Only one of his single-authored plays, *The Life of Sir John Oldcastle*, survives. As we shall see, Drayton shaped his later literary career in quite an ambitious and upmarket manner. Both men wrote in a wide variety of poetic genres. Drayton specialized in pastoral verse, love poetry and versified English history and topography, while Jonson's chief bent was towards courtly epigrams and satires.

Both Drayton and Jonson made many explicit literary dedications to courtly patrons, including some notable aristocratic ladies. Female patrons were likely to have had considerably more leisure in which to focus on favoured poets than did their husbands, and

BEN: IOHNSON II. ✳ VERA EFFIGIES DOCTISSIMI POETARVM ANGLORVM

Ro: Vaughan fecit.

Johnsoni typus, ecce! qui furoris,
Antistes sacer, Enthei, Camenis,
Vindex Ingenÿ recens Sepulti,
Antiquæ reparator vnus artis,

Defuncta Pater Eruditionis,
Et Scenæ veteris novator audax.
Nec fælix minus, aut minus politus
Cui solus similis, Figura, viv et.

O could there be an art found out that might
Produce his shape soe lively as to Write. Ab: Holl
Are to be Sould by C William Peake

9 Engraved portrait of Ben
Jonson by Robert Vaughan,
1640.

may also have been more inclined to commission visual images as mementoes. This may help to explain why several portraits of these two men – both engraved and painted – survive from their lifetimes (FIG. 9). Shakespeare's attested patrons were all male, and even the otherwise mysterious 'M[aster] W.H.' to whom he dedicated his sonnets in 1609 may at least be assumed to have been male. Another factor may be the longer lifespans of Drayton and Jonson. While Shakespeare died, perhaps rather suddenly, and certainly in provincial Stratford, at just 52, Drayton lived to 68. Jonson, despite a lifetime of heavy drinking, survived to 65. An extra decade and more of life may have enabled these two writers to achieve more widespread personal fame within their lifetimes than Shakespeare was able to do.

A further particular feature shared by Drayton and Jonson is that they were represented as crowned with laurel, either while alive or when only very recently deceased. Shakespeare, whose receding hairline would have been much improved aesthetically by the addition of a crown of laurel, is shown bare-headed even in the portrait that accompanies the First Folio. This is not the least among the many peculiarities that mark Shakespeare's image and career as exceptional, and is in many respects rather puzzling.

Drayton seems to have been especially adept in securing the friendly patronage of ladies. Much of his early poetry was dedicated to Anne Goodere, later Lady Rainsford. She was the implied object of amorous devotion in Drayton's much revised sonnet sequence *Ideas Mirror*, of which later versions were entitled simply *Idea*. The connection began with Drayton's earliest attested patron, Henry Goodere of Polesworth, within whose household he was probably brought up and educated. Drayton dedicated his poem *Matilda* to Lucy Harington, soon to become countess of Bedford and a famously generous patroness, shortly before her marriage. There is a portrait miniature believed by some to depict Drayton, attributed to Peter Oliver, apparently painted within Drayton's lifetime. It is now in the collection of the duke of Portland. This seems likely to have been commissioned by one of Drayton's female patrons, such as Mary (Curzon), countess of Dorset.[11]

Drayton's ability both to secure and to retain upmarket female patronage seems to have endured to the end of his life and even beyond. Though he apparently died in modest circumstances, in London, he was very splendidly commemorated after his death. As Adam White has recently shown, it was probably the countess of Dorset, a learned lady who acted as governess to the future King Charles II, who commissioned and paid for Drayton's remarkably opulent monument in Westminster Abbey, located in what is now called Poets' Corner.[12] She may also have been responsible for the wording on the monument which commemorates Michael Drayton as 'A MEMORABLE POET OF THIS AGE, EXCHANGED HIS LAURELL FOR A CROWNE OF GLORYE ANNO 1631.'

In its design, in its material substance – marble – and above all in its Westminster Abbey location, Drayton's monument is far more splendid and conspicuous than Shakespeare's monument in Holy Trinity, Stratford-upon-Avon. This now seems ironic since few visitors to Westminster Abbey are likely to be familiar with Drayton's poetry, while most will be familiar with some of the works of Shakespeare – or, at the very least, with Shakespeare's name.

Jonson, too, was adept in securing courtly patronage, some of which was derived from aristocratic ladies. For instance, *The Alchemist*, probably his best-known play, was dedicated to Lady Mary Wroth in 1616. She was a niece of Sir Philip Sidney and the daughter of his brother Robert. He also addressed two flattering poems to her in his *Epigrams*.[13] He wrote a flattering verse letter to Philip Sidney's daughter Elizabeth, newly married and countess of Rutland, in 1610. Among other compliments, he wished her soon to produce a male heir – being unfortunately unaware that her marriage was unconsummated. The poem was later printed in a revised version. It is not clear, however, that either of these ladies commissioned images of Jonson, who was ridiculed for his unattractive appearance in Thomas Dekker's satiric play *Satiromastix* in 1601/2. Here, two contrasting pictures are brought on stage by Captain Tucca. In an obvious echo of the celebrated 'bedchamber' scene in *Hamlet* in which Hamlet compels his mother to 'Look here, upon this picture, and on this', a contrast is drawn between the two portraits shown on stage. One represents 'the Roman poet Horace, who had a trim long-beard, and a reasonable good face for a Poet', while that of Jonson, who claims to be a reincarnation of Horace, shows him as hideously pockmarked, haggard and 'villainous' in appearance. Highly uncomplimentary to Jonson though it may be, this passage suggests that his face was well known to many audience members, both from existing portraits and from eyewitness sightings of the man himself. He had a habit of attending performances of his own plays. Also, by the time of Dekker's *Satiromastix*, Jonson was notorious for having killed a fellow actor, Gabriel Spencer, in October 1598, an incident which may be recalled in the description of his looks as 'villainous': Jonson was a convicted felon. Though he escaped execution, he was deprived of his possessions and branded on the fleshy part of the thumb of his right hand. This ensured that he could never again be delivered from penal execution by pleading benefit of clergy – that is, receiving pardon on the grounds of classical learning. It is striking that Robert Vaughan's engraved portrait of Jonson – dated 1640, just three years after Jonson's death – shows the poet holding a glove in his left hand. Only the top half of his right arm is shown, leaving the branded right hand invisible.

Jonson's social prominence as a striking and assertive personality, especially familiar to Londoners, as well as a learned and

versatile writer, may have led to an interest in his physical appearance that was distinctly stronger than interest in Shakespeare's.
From the later 1590s onwards the latter was known above all for
his plays, works that figured many and varied characters, none
of whom could be seen as portraits of the author. Furthermore,
Shakespeare does not seem to have been at the centre of any kind
of literary clique or club, as Jonson was in his latter years. Yet
another reason why Jonson was depicted as a laureate, crowned
with bay leaves, may be that in 1619 he was awarded honorary
degrees by both Oxford and Cambridge.[14] Had Shakespeare lived
a few years longer, he too might conceivably have been awarded
an Oxford degree as Jonson was, through the favour of the generous patron William Herbert, earl of Pembroke, then Oxford's
chancellor. But his relatively limited classical attainments might
have precluded this. It is not clear that Shakespeare could have
delivered an acceptance speech in Latin.

Shakespeare, then, was different from all of his poet contemporaries in many respects, including that of portraiture. Though
two likenesses of him, both in sculpture and engraving, were on
view by 1623, unlike those of his contemporaries these portraits
were most likely to have been made posthumously, about seven
years after his death. Moreover, as we shall see, few admirers of
his writings have been satisfied by them.

TWO

The Stratford bust

THE MONUMENT TO Shakespeare mounted on the north wall of the chancel of Holy Trinity Church, Stratford-upon-Avon, was there by the spring of 1623, just seven years after his death. It seems reasonable to hope, therefore, that this likeness has every chance of being an accurate portrayal of Shakespeare. Unfortunately, however, the history of the monument is rather complex, and it is not clear whether it is based on a likeness made while Shakespeare was alive. Also, the verses that appear on the monument are anonymous, though there are various individuals known to Shakespeare who could have composed such an epitaph.

We know that the monument was in place by 1623 because of an allusion to it in an even more significant Shakespeare memorial, the First Folio edition of Shakespeare's plays. The monument is mentioned in the opening lines of a poem by Leonard Digges prefacing the First Folio:

TO THE MEMORIE
Of the deceased Authour Maister
W. SHAKESPEARE.

Shake-speare, *at length thy pious fellowes give*
The world thy Workes: thy Workes, by which, out-live
Thy Tombe, thy name must: when that stone is rent,
And Time dissolves thy Stratford *Moniment,*
Here we alive shall view thee still.

10 (*previous spread*)
The Stratford bust of Shakespeare on the north wall of Holy Trinity Church, Stratford-upon-Avon.

Leonard Digges appears to have known Shakespeare quite well. His stepfather was Thomas Russell, a close friend of Shakespeare whom the poet chose as the chief overseer of his will. Russell lived in Alderminster, only a couple of miles south of Stratford. Digges was therefore in an excellent position to be aware that the tasks, first, of procuring texts of Shakespeare's plays – whether printed or in manuscript – and, later, of assembling the volume's preliminary material, including its frontispiece, had taken some years. This is suggested by the phrase 'at length'. As we shall see, Digges was more prescient than he knew in foreseeing the fragility of Shakespeare's 'Tombe' in contrast to the durability of his 'Workes' and 'name'. The physical 'Moniment' lasted barely a quarter-century before becoming in need of repair.

Half-length, wall-mounted monuments had become extremely popular by the early 1600s. Indeed, M.H. Spielmann, author of what is still the most detailed study of the Stratford bust, describes this type of memorial as having become 'almost a hackneyed form of sepulchral monument' by about 1600. According to Brian Kemp, 'The later C16 in effect invented the hanging wall monument, that is, a monument not standing upon the floor, but wholly suspended on the wall into which it is fixed by mortar and iron ties.'[1] A major reason for the popularity of this form of monument was that it was comparatively cheap, and thus appealed to 'a wide circle of clients of middling rank'. Strictly speaking, however, although wall-mounted figures are commonly alluded to as busts, they often depict 'the entire upper third, half or more of the figure'.[2] Since most previous writers on Shakespeare have described the Stratford effigy as a bust, I shall retain that term for simplicity's sake (FIG. 10).

Shakespeare's monument is made up of at least five distinct sculptured components, not including such smaller additional parts as the inscribed plaque beneath the alcove, the pen and paper held by the deceased, and the chapless skull (i.e. lacking a jaw-bone) that perches on top of the whole structure. All of the larger components were probably fashioned in the Johnson[3] workshop in Southwark before being transported from London to Stratford. The largest and heaviest piece is the frame, made of black and white alabaster. The centrepiece is the effigy, designed to fit within the alcove. Two symbolic naked boys were carved and placed to sit on small mounds of earth on either side of the top of the frame, each boy and his mound being carved from a single piece of stone. Finally, nowadays very dark and grimy but originally no doubt splendidly bright with gold and silver leaf, the uppermost sculptured item is the Shakespeare coat of arms, fully displayed with mantling and crest, all carved in relief on an altar-like cube of stone with a pediment above. The heraldic bird that is Shakespeare's crest now looks like a black crow, and is in desperate need of cleaning and resilvering. As is shown in documents still surviving in the archives of the College of Arms, this was originally designed as a silver falcon with wings widely outspread in a posture known to falconers as 'the shaking' – the movement a bird of prey makes just before it takes flight. It holds a gold and silver spear, punning on the surname 'Shake Spear'. The single item lacking from the carved and painted coat of arms in Holy Trinity is the motto devised in October 1596: *Non sanz droict* – that is, in heraldic French, 'Not without right'. It implies that the holder of this coat of arms is fully entitled to display it. The motto may have been eliminated from use early on, in accordance with Shakespeare's own instructions, because of the mockery it had received, especially from Ben Jonson.[4] In his 1599 comedy *Every Man out of His Humour*, Jonson describes a ridiculously over-elaborate coat of arms purchased by a rich but dim-witted rustic. It featured a boar's head with the motto *Not without Mustard*.

Each of the five sculptured pieces needed to be very carefully packed and wadded, probably with straw, before being transported by barge up the Thames from Southwark as far as Oxford. In this period, according to Nigel Llewellyn, 'The Thames allowed river transport up-stream beyond Reading.' His useful map suggests that it usually continued to be navigable as far as Oxford, after which the remainder of the journey – in this instance, from Oxford to Stratford – would have to be made overland, more slowly and expensively, by cart or wagon.[5] Llewellyn also observes that 'Tomb-makers were wary of carriage costs, since monuments were heavy, bulky and fragile, and whenever they could they used familiar modes of water transport.'[6] At the point where sculptures had to be transported by land either the patron or the patron's servants normally assumed responsibility both for logistics and for payment. The patrons in this instance are likely to have been Shakespeare's primary heirs, Dr John Hall and his wife Susanna, née Shakespeare. Their servants, or assistants, may have included Shakespeare's best-loved colleagues and friends, some of whom were also working on the parallel task of assembling texts of all of Shakespeare's plays.

This scenario may provide an explanation for a fascinating discovery made by the late Mary Edmond.[7] According to the Churchwardens' Accounts of St Martin's, Carfax, John Heminges spent some time in Oxford in 1620, in the course of which he made a generous donation of 10 shillings towards the restoration of Carfax Tower, still a central monument in the city. Mary Edmond suggested that Heminges was in Oxford en route for Stratford, and in pursuit of play-texts in New Place. This may indeed be the case. In addition – though Heminges is most fully recorded as a Londoner, a family man, a loyal parishioner and eventually a churchwarden of St Mary's, Aldermanbury – he had grown up in Droitwich, Worcestershire, less than twenty miles from

Stratford. He may well have continued to have family connections in those parts. An additional possibility is that Heminges's
presence in Oxford was connected to the process of receiving the
components of the Shakespeare monument after their arrival by
water, and overseeing their safe transfer from barge to wagon for
the forty-mile overland journey to Stratford. Following the rather
sudden death of Richard Burbage, in March 1619, Heminges was
the senior surviving member of the trio of close friends and colleagues commemorated by Shakespeare in his will.[8] All three men
may have concerned themselves both with Shakespeare's stone
monument, sculpted in Southwark, near the Globe, and with his
literary remains during the period immediately following his death.

Not only was the monument composed of different parts, to be
assembled and finally secured *in situ* in Holy Trinity, Stratford; the
parts themselves were made from a variety of materials. The frame
and alcove are carved from white marble, black marble being used
for the two Corinthian columns on either side of the alcove and
black touchstone for the inlaid panels. The bust is described by
Schoenbaum as being 'carved from soft bluish Cotswold limestone'.
Spielmann describes the material as 'limestone from the neighbour-
hood of Stroud – a soft stone in common use when the sculpture
was to be coloured'. According, once again, to Spielmann, the effigy
lacks detailed modelling of facial features 'because the colour would
be left to do its work – the eyebrows so lightly chiselled that they
hardly suggest the hair; and in the open mouth the teeth without
divisions, in the band, which is painted white'.

Perhaps this strategy is where the trouble began. The granular
texture of limestone is, I imagine, effective in absorbing strong
applications of paint, but not sufficiently smooth to permit much
delicacy of line or shading. Most varieties of Cotswold limestone
are notoriously subject to erosion and decay. This may be seen
in the example of the seventeen (originally thirteen) super-sized

heads of Roman emperors that encircle the Sheldonian Theatre in Oxford. These were originally carved from Headington freestone, a form of limestone derived from petrified coral. The heads lasted only from 1669 to 1868, when they were replaced with Headington freestone. This time they seem to have decayed even more quickly, perhaps because of additional pollution from smoke and car fumes. They were replaced for the second time in 1972, this time using a more durable form of stone, Clipsham, quarried in Rutland. The splendid heads, which continue to look pretty fine, were newly designed and carved by Michael Black. While the Stratford bust has never, so far as we know, been completely replaced with new work, as the Oxford emperors have been, it too has undergone numerous physical interventions in the cause of restoration.

Many lovers of Shakespeare's works in modern times have greatly disliked the image of Shakespeare presented by the Stratford bust. Professor John Dover Wilson even claimed that 'this bust is one of the greatest of all obstacles to the true understanding of Shakespeare …[it] might suit well enough with an affluent and retired butcher, but does gross wrong to the dead poet.'[9]

One of several major flaws in Dover Wilson's claim derives from two assumptions: first, that it is essential for a 'great poet' to look like one; and, second, that we are all generally agreed on what that would entail. Since the invention of photography we have become rather more accustomed to the idea that writers don't necessarily conform to any generally agreed notion of how we would expect them to look.

A further flaw is Dover Wilson's assumption that the effigy, as it has appeared in Holy Trinity, Stratford, during the past century, is a reliable guide to its original appearance. The bust as we see it now is at so many removes from its original condition – after repeated attempts to restore, and on some occasions to improve it – that it is impossible to say quite what its original appearance may have been. Did it always seem slightly clumsy, provincial and artistically second-rate, or may it have been quite a handsome effigy when brand new?

Images of the bust and restoration

The earliest image we have of the Stratford bust is an engraving made by Wenceslas Hollar at the behest of William Dugdale. This was included as an illustration in Dugdale's study of Warwickshire published in 1656 (FIG. 11). As Spielmann pointed out, this image is manifestly inaccurate, even though it was engraved by the much admired Hollar:

> We see the poor design of the shield and mantling, the ridiculous boys cut off their mounds and perched insecurely on the edge of the cornice … the one holding aloft a spade, and the other an hour-glass … The arch is of a different form, perhaps to allow the wide space necessary for the unauthentic stuck-out elbows of the figure. The portrait is no portrait at all: it shows us a sickly, decrepit old gentleman, with a falling moustache, much more than fifty-two years old.

Finally, rather than showing the playwright in the act of writing, holding a quill with his right hand while smoothing down a sheet of paper with his left, in Hollar's version 'both hands are here upon a cushion which, for no reason except perhaps abdominal pains, is hugged against what dancing-masters euphemistically term "the lower chest".'[10] Hollar did not visit Stratford-upon-Avon, but based his image on a sketch made by someone else, presumably Dugdale. Anyway, he was in the habit of handling his compositions rather freely, changing details as he saw fit.[11] Also, even if Hollar's engraving could be shown to be accurate, the original sketch was made some time after 1649, when the bust underwent its first restoration, being 're-beautified' to counteract the effects of

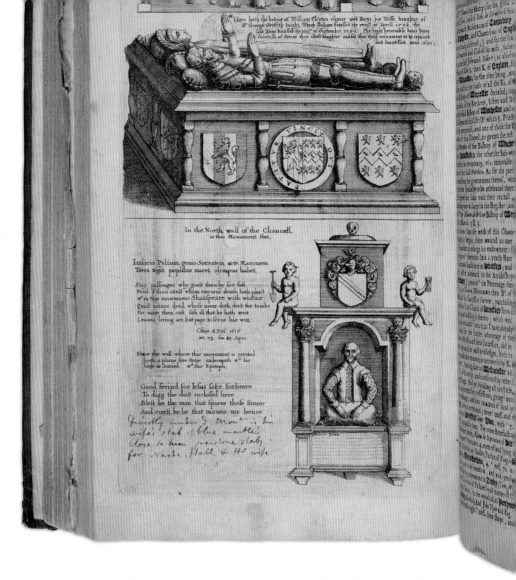

11 Engraving of the Stratford bust made by Wenceslas Hollar for William Dugdale, *The Antiquities of Warwickshire* (1656). Gough Warw. 22.

damp.[12] Unfortunately, it was the Dugdale–Hollar image that was used as the model for many later engravings, with further inaccuracies and absurdities being added by artists, none of whom had gone to the trouble of travelling to Stratford to compare Hollar's image with the original monument. In a late-eighteenth-century engraving by Charles Grignion, for instance, the left-hand boy, the one who should supposedly represent Labour, holds an arrow as if he were Cupid, the little god of love. He also appears to perch very precariously on the corner of the monument, balancing on a single buttock.

If Spielmann's scenario is correct, the original scheme may have been to use a fairly standard, lightly modelled head, whose porous stone made it possible to add fine detail and subtleties of skin tone, beard and facial expression by means of skilful painting. All of these were continually damaged by the passage of time, and then damaged further by being overpainted. The very worst offender here was a man who was distinguished as a major, and in other respects mostly admirable, editor of Shakespeare's writings: Edmond Malone (1741–1812). He should have known better.

In 1793, with the support of the Revd James Davenport, then vicar of Holy Trinity, Malone paid for the effigy to be painted white all over, thus making it appear more 'classical', while also returning it to what Malone apparently believed was its original state. He was probably not aware that many ancient Roman statues, even when sculpted from white marble, were originally painted and coloured. As Samuel Schoenbaum remarked, 'No other act of Malone's did such lasting damage to his reputation as his tampering with the Stratford bust.'[13]

Horror at the white overpainting of the bust was widespread as well as long lasting. As Schoenbaum, again, reported: 'Victor Hugo, in exile on Guernsey, remembered the desecration. "An imbecile, Malone", he wrote in his *William Shakespeare*, "made commentaries on his plays, and, as a logical sequence, whitewashed his tomb".'[14] Malone may have had a further motive. As mentioned above, the bust, already showing signs of damp and decay, had been 're-beautified' – that is to say, lavishly restored – as early as 1649. Nearly a century later, in 1746, it had been entirely recoloured yet again by a painter called John Hall. He was no relation, so far as we know, of Shakespeare's son-in-law Dr John Hall, who had died in 1635. The combined effect of damage done to the original colouring, followed first by lavish touching-up (1649) and then by a complete repainting (1746) which was, as Spielmann clearly demonstrates, done on the cheap, seems to have produced a coarse and garish image. This is suggested by the depiction of the whole monument by the painter John Hall. To Malone's fastidious eyes, the image may well have appeared vulgar and clumsy, something that a full coat of fresh white paint ought, in his opinion, to mitigate.

Yet more interference and restoration ensued: 'In 1861 the white-lead paint was removed with solvents by Simon Collins, and the damaged paint underneath boldly and summarily restored in its proper colours, though in too high a key.'[15] Given the porous nature of limestone, such a procedure – and especially the application of solvents – must have done yet more damage to the surface of the effigy, and removed it even further from its original painting and modelling.

The whole history of the Stratford bust, from 1649 onwards, is one of overzealous interference and horribly ill-judged and mismanaged attempts at restoration. It is particularly striking that while the Shakespeare monument has endured repeated intervention, with consequent damage and the destruction of reliable evidence for its original appearance, the adjacent monument to John Combe, which had been carved in the very same workshop only two years earlier, 'has never had to be touched, and is in a sound condition' – at least in 1924, the time when Spielmann was writing. A high price was paid for Shakespeare's celebrity and the consequent development of Stratford tourism.

In addition to Hollar's unsatisfactory and inaccurate engraving of the Stratford bust, there is just one other eyewitness image of it that precedes the 1746 painting. This is a sketch drawn by George Vertue in 1737 that shows the rear view of an admiring and well-dressed gentleman who stands on the gravestone that

Rev. Mr. Kendrick Minister there. non

Mr. Harbord Statuary lives there at Stratford
and I commissiond him to make me a Cast
from the Bust of Shakespears head on his Mont.

no. 1.
on Shakespeers
grave Stone near the
rails of the commu-
table.

Good frend for Jesus sake forbeare.
to digg the dust enclosed Heare
blest be the Man that Spares these Stones
and Curst behe yt. moves my bones,

heleft 2 daughters
Susanna daughter of
Shakespeare, married to John Hall
Gent:

another Daughter married to
Mr. Nash. of ----

o. 2. his wifes
grave Stone.
nne .... wife of
Shakespeare dyd.
aug. 6. 1623.

covered Anne Hathaway's remains as he gazes at the Shakespeare monument (FIG. 12). It is broadly correct in terms of the overall outline and position of the monument. However, it leaves a blank space where the coat of arms should be, and shows the poet's head rather as it appears in the so-called 'Chandos' oil painting, with a finely tapering chin and pointed beard, and a pleasing absence of that puddingy look that makes the Stratford bust – at least, in the form in which it has reached us – so unattractive. Overall, however, Vertue's drawing is so light and so lacking in fine detail that it belongs to the history of Shakespeare's literary reputation, the great fame that was beginning to bring tourists to Stratford, rather than to that of his effigy.

12 George Vertue, *Sketch of a Visitor Admiring the Stratford Bust* (1737). London, British Library, Portland Loan 29/246, 17.

Design and inscription

Disappointing though the Stratford bust may be, both as a work of art and as a pleasing likeness, there is still interest to be derived from the monument's overall design. This may reflect instructions delivered by the poet himself when alive. He drafted his will in January 1616, revising it radically on 25 March, after his younger daughter Judith had married the unsatisfactory Thomas Quiney. Though only the second, revised, version, survives, the fact that an earlier version existed strongly suggests that Shakespeare was already ailing in January, in which case he had several weeks in which to think about his apparently impending death. In this period most men made their wills only when it seemed that death was clearly in view. There is a negative feature of the monument that conforms closely to the spirit in which he dictated the last version of his will, omitting all mention of his wife until a very late, minimal, afterthought – with the bequest of the celebrated 'second-best bed'. The Stratford bust, comparably, appears to be in no sense a family monument, but a memorial to a singular and exceptionally brilliant individual.

Many Jacobean wall monuments represent, or at least allude to, the spouses and children of the deceased. An extreme example, close in time to Shakespeare's monument, is the wall-mounted monument to Richard Chernocke in Hulcote, Bedfordshire. This shows the dead man with 'His father and his two wives with their children ... in the form of a tall standing wall monument of three tiers containing no fewer than 29 kneeling effigies.'[16]

In total contrast, it is notable that on the Stratford monument no mention is made of Shakespeare's wife, daughters, sons-in-law or granddaughter. The verses on the plaque immediately below the effigy read thus:

IUDICIO PYLIUM GENIO SOCRATEM, ARTE MARONEM,
TERRA TEGIT, POPULUS MAERET, OLYMPUS HABET.

STAY PASSENGER,[17] WHY GOEST THOU BY SO FAST,
READ IF THOU CANST, WHOM ENVIOUS[18] DEATH HATH PLAST
WITH IN THIS MONUMENT SHAKSPEARE: WITH WHOME
QUICK NATURE DIDE[19] WHOSE NAME DOTH DECK THIS TOMBE,
FAR MORE, THEN COST: SIEH[20] ALL, THAT HE HATH WRITT,
LEAVES LIVING ART, BUT PAGE, TO SERVE HIS WITT.

OBIIT ANNO DOMINI 1616
AETATIS 53 DIE 23 APRILIS[21]

The two Latin lines that open the epitaph may be translated, in reverse order from the original, as 'Olympus possesses, the people lament, the earth covers, [a man who was] in artistry a Virgil ['Maro'], in brilliance a Socrates, in wisdom a Nestor' (FIG. 13). The author of these lines is unknown. It is possible that Shakespeare's son-in-law, Dr John Hall, was sufficiently well educated to have composed some epigrammatic lines of Latin verse, but there is no reason to suppose that he was particularly interested in poetry. Given that the monument is decidedly not a family memorial, but rather one that celebrates and commemorates the dead man's unique brilliance as a writer, I am more inclined to

13 The plaque beneath the Stratford bust in Holy Trinity Church, Stratford-upon-Avon.

associate the entire epitaph with some member of Shakespeare's social circle who is on record as taking a close interest in his writings. Thomas Russell's Oxford-educated son Leonard Digges, for instance, undoubtedly wrote two published poems commemorating Shakespeare and his writings.[22] Shakespeare's old friend and long-term playing-company colleague John Heminges – the man who may have overseen part of the bust's original journey to Stratford – must also have known Shakespeare's plays exceptionally well through performance. Either of these men would be considerably better qualified than Dr John Hall to pay tribute to Shakespeare in verse as an embodiment of 'quick nature' – a writer whose brilliant fluency was informed by natural insight and eloquence, rather than painfully squeezed out through hard study and a conventional academic education. The extravagantly high claims made here for Shakespeare's wisdom and intellectual insight would also come more naturally from someone who had worked alongside him, or had encountered his work directly in performance, rather than from a son-in-law who encountered him chiefly in a domestic setting.

In combination, the Latin superscription and English verse suggest that Shakespeare's name and fame were both greatly celebrated and widely dispersed even before the landmark publication of the First Folio in 1623. The Latin superscription makes grand claims for him as a world-class genius – and he is indeed widely acknowledged as such today. The closing pun on the word 'page' at the end of the English verse seems, in its almost comic grotesqueness, distinctly Shakespearean in manner. Paper pages inscribed by later, younger, writers can aspire only to a different form of pagehood, confined to the status of junior servitors to their now dead master.

Whoever composed the English verse on the monument was probably familiar with the *Sonnets*, and especially with lines 9–12 of Sonnet 108, the concluding item in the 'fair youth' sequence, according to which

> eternal love, in love's fresh case
> Weighs not the dust and injury of age,
> Nor gives to necessary wrinkles place
> But makes antiquity for aye his page.

The general sense here is that 'true love' can transcend both the ravages of time and the ageing process, and makes 'antiquity' – alluding here both to ancient times and to old men – for ever 'fresh', relegating other love, however ancient, to the lowly status of a page. My own view is that the likeliest author of the words on the monument is Leonard Digges, an attested poet, scholar and translator, and a senior resident, latterly, of University College, Oxford.

There are other ways in which the Stratford bust is unusual. For instance, though it has often been connected to the genre, this is not a scholar's monument, strictly speaking. Shakespeare is not shown surrounded by books and manuscripts, as is, for instance, John Stow, whose 1605 marble monument in St Andrew Undershaft in the City of London (FIG. 14) was constructed by Nicholas Johnson (of the Johnson workshop in Southwark). It has frequently been compared with Shakespeare's.[23] While Stow gazes intently downwards, hard at work on his *Chronicle*, Shakespeare is shown as having just written something that he immediately proceeds, actor-like, to deliver orally, facing his audience with lips slightly parted. Rather than being scholarly or academic, Shakespeare's writing is very close to speech, consisting of lines to be delivered to listeners. He appears as a single and unique genius who has no peers among his contemporaries, only among the ancients.

The Stratford monument is also unusual in its lack of even minimal or formulaic declarations of religious devotion. Many

effigies show the deceased kneeling in prayer, or suggest the dead person's inclination towards piety and humility in other ways, with downcast eyes, and perhaps an inscription which testifies to the subject's devotion to God. This monument, conversely, shows its subject boldly confronting the viewer, quite sure of himself and confident of the power of his own achievements. His directness of gaze is both unusual and a little disconcerting.

However, in contrast to the monument's celebration of the subject's unique brilliance and strong 'presence' when alive, there are features that clearly function as a *memento mori*, embodying unsparing reminders that the man whose remains lie below has indeed died, and in that respect now shares the common lot of all. Skulls are not a particularly common feature of early Jacobean funeral monuments, but this one has two, both chapless – without a lower jaw. I am tempted to wonder whether the topmost skull, above the coat of arms, may allude to William Shakespeare's unique entitlement to the arms. His hard-won coat will not be assumed after his death by a son. If this reading has anything in it, we may have Shakespeare's only surviving allusion to the death of his son Hamnet in 1596.

Labour and Rest, and the Johnson workshop

The two curly-haired boys representing Labour and Rest who sit on mounds of earth, one holding a spade, the other an extinguished torch, are also an unusual feature. I am aware of only four other monuments that include figures of Labour and Rest, though there may be more. All of them are Jacobean, and all appear to be associated with the Johnson workshop in Southwark. Whether they should be seen as carrying any meaning specific to the deceased, or whether they were simply images that had become fashionable in the early Jacobean period, I am not qualified to judge.

14 The monument to the chronicler John Stow in St Andrew Undershaft Church, City of London.

The earliest example of which I am aware is the monument to Elizabeth South, who died in 1604. Her grieving husband commissioned a fine alabaster monument in St Faith's, Kelstern, Lincolnshire, which is illustrated in Llewellyn's book.[24] The boy on the left, who represents Labour, rests his foot on a spade, while the right-hand boy holds a downturned torch supported by the top of a skull. Their meaning is made clear by brief Latin inscriptions: for the boy with the spade *Nil sine labore* – that is, 'Nothing [is achieved] without toil'; and for the boy with the extinguished torch *In alto requies* – 'Repose is on high [in heaven]'. As a further *memento mori*, Elizabeth South rests her left foot on another skull.

15 Boy representing Labour, from the monument to Thomas Sutton in the chapel of the Charterhouse, London.

My second and third examples both have striking links with Shakespeare. The second is the opulent and highly ornamented monument to Thomas Sutton in the chapel of the London Charterhouse. His unprecedently lavish bequest transformed the Charterhouse – which had been a Carthusian monastery in pre-Reformation times – from an exceptionally grand Elizabethan mansion, which belonged latterly to Thomas Howard, earl of Suffolk, into an upmarket almshouse and grammar school. Sutton's bequest had come as something of a surprise both to his kin and to the City fathers, so there was considerable delay before the monument was planned.[25] It was not fully completed until 1615, bringing it very

16 Boy representing Rest, from the monument to Thomas Sutton in the chapel of the Charterhouse, London.

close to the time when one of the very same company of sculptors was commissioned to commemorate Shakespeare. Its construction is exceptionally well documented from records that remain in the archives of the Charterhouse. These leave no room for doubt that the monument was carved by a team of sculptors led by Nicholas Johnson in partnership with two other outstanding sculptors of the time, Edmund Kinsman and Nicholas Stone. Their combined fee came to the tremendous sum of £400.

This monument is astonishingly richly ornamented, with large female figures embodying virtues – Faith, Hope, Peace and Plenty – as well as a very detailed frieze in low relief that depicts the (future) brothers of the Charterhouse on the right and troops of well-behaved and well-dressed schoolboys on the left. The ornamentation is so profuse that the two small boys up aloft who symbolize Labour and Rest may not at first attract the viewer's attention, perhaps registering simply as decorative putti. However, they are fine examples of the genre, carved in marble (FIGS 14 & 15). Each plump and curly-headed boy stands upright, the one on the viewer's left holding a spade, the right-hand one an extinguished torch resting on a skull, almost exactly as on the monument to Elizabeth South. It seems highly likely that the relatively modest Shakespeare monument, probably commissioned on the basis of a much smaller budget and constructed by the Johnsons – perhaps no more than a year or two later – was influenced by the Sutton monument in terms of its inclusion of these symbolic figures. The very same craftsman may have been responsible for the figures of Labour and Rest, though Shakespeare's are different in being seated, rather than standing, probably for the mundane reason that this monument is too small to accommodate standing figures.

Finally, the spectacular monument to Roger Manners, 5th earl of Rutland, in St Mary's, Bottesford, Rutland, provides a link

to Shakespeare of a quite different kind. As we shall see, Roger
Manners's younger brother Francis, the 6th earl, had been a late
patron of Shakespeare. Francis Manners succeeded to the earldom
on 26 June 1612, and is described in the *Oxford Dictionary of National Biography* as having been 'already active in masques and tilts
[tournaments] at court'.[26] Rutland's patronage of Shakespeare has
been largely overlooked, or at least remarkably little discussed,
by biographers. Strangely, it is not mentioned in the *ODNB*
entries either for Rutland or for Shakespeare. The evidence for it
is to be found among the Rutland manuscripts in Belvoir Castle.[27]
On 31 March 1613 the new earl's steward recorded two payments
of 44 shillings in gold, one 'to m*aste*r Shakspeare' for 'my lordes
impreso'; the other 'To Richard Burbadge for paynting & making
yt'. An *impreso* or, more correctly, an *impresa* was a complex visual
and verbal device combining a motto with an image. Together,
these commented on the character and aspirations of the courtier
who bore it, usually in a tournament. The meaning was meant to
be quite hard to decipher. Attempting to read, or decode, *imprese*
was one of the features that made royal tournaments uniquely
exciting and fascinating for courtly spectators, especially ladies.
Though each tilter's face was concealed by a helmet, his identity
and aspirations were ingeniously coded both in the colours he
wore and, more riddlingly, in the *impresa* that he bore on a shield.

In 1631 Shakespeare had already had some experience in de-
vising *imprese* for use in the theatre. His popular tragi-comedy
Pericles, written in collaboration with George Wilkins in 1607/8,
included a tournament scene (2.2) that features a parade of six
knights, each with a painted shield and cryptic motto. Perhaps
Burbage, known to be a skilful painter, had prepared the shields
deployed in early productions of *Pericles*. These may well have
been viewed by the theatre-loving Francis Manners. The fee
of 44 shillings was handsome, and the twofold payment of this

sum – in gold, at that – suggests that Rutland anticipated a very
good result from Shakespeare and Burbage's joint work. He was
evidently satisfied, since he paid an even larger sum – this time
to Burbage alone – for another painted *impresa* on 31 March 1616:
'for my Lordes shelde and for the embleame £4 18s. ... [for] ...
my Lordes tilting on 25th March'.[28] This time, sadly, Shakespeare
was not able to contribute to the work, for he was on his bed of
sickness in faraway Stratford, dying just under four weeks later.
It seems safe to assume that Rutland would have employed him
again had he been available.

Rutland's 1613 *impresa* was devised for his participation, as a
newly acceded earl, in the Jacobean Accession Day Tilt – the most
splendid tournament of the year, held on 24 March 1613. His interest in visual display and spectacle is reflected more permanently in
the exceptional lavishness of the monument that he commissioned
for his late brother in 1617, which is well documented: 'Paid to
Nycholas Johnson, tomb maker, in full payment for the finishinge
of the monument erected at Botesforth for the late Earle Roger
of Rutland, £100; there having ben formerly paied £50 in full
paiment of the agreement of £150.'[29]

The latest edition of the *Leicestershire and Rutland* volume of
Nikolaus Pevsner's *Buildings of England* includes this typically
brief and unenthusiastic comment on the monument to the 5th
earl: 'Between additional columns at the sides, clumsy figures of
Labour and Rest.'[30]

What have not been much noticed are either the fact that the
6th earl of Rutland had been personally acquainted with Shakespeare, or that there are distinctive motifs – those two symbolic
boys – that connect the 5th earl's magnificent monument to
Shakespeare's very much more modest one, probably constructed
within the same time span, 1617–19.

Despite its poor physical condition and limited merits as a work of art, the Stratford bust undoubtedly makes a statement. A major reason for its artistic shortcomings may be that Shakespeare never had sufficient leisure to pose for a really first-rate painting that would have provided a good facial likeness for subsequent artists to copy. I shall explore this further in the next chapter, and in Chapter 4 I shall examine a portrait that, though very attractive, may have required relatively little 'sitting' time. Probably in accordance with his own wishes, however, Shakespeare is shown in the bust as a gentleman of exceptional strength and distinction whose status is acknowledged both in the town of his birth and in a much wider world. He resembles his own late anti-hero Coriolanus in seeing himself as solely responsible for his own very considerable achievements: 'Alone I did it' (*Coriolanus* 5.6.117).

As suggested by the remark in the verses on the monument that with Shakespeare's death, 'quick Nature dide', the poet-player's life was exceptionally active and productive – more powered with creative energy and fluency than we can ever fully glean from his surviving writings. According to his faithful friends John Heminges and Henry Condell, editors of the 1623 First Folio collection of his plays, 'as he was a happie imitator of Nature, [he] was a most gentle expresser of it. His mind and hand went together: and what he thought, he uttered with that easinesse, that we have scarce received from him a blot in his papers.'

Not only was Shakepeare's own art exceptionally realistic, and close to 'Nature'; its realism – or naturalism – is affirmed as unsurpassable. Though awkwardly expressed, the verses on the monument pay a tribute that does not seem excessive even now. There are few other writers whose fame and pre-eminence have endured continuously for more than four centuries.

Mr. WILLIAM
SHAKESPEARES

COMEDIES,
HISTORIES, &
TRAGEDIES.

Published according to the True Originall Copies.

Martin Droeshout sculpsit London.

LONDON

Printed by Isaac Iaggard, and Ed. Blount. 1623.

THREE

The Droeshout engraving

EVEN WITHIN HIS lifetime the high artistic status accorded to Shakespeare, together with the great popularity of some of his plays, ensured that he attracted admirers who wanted to know what he looked like. Awareness of this during the years immediately following Shakespeare's death in 1616 presumably lies behind the decision by John Heminges and Henry Condell, the volume's editors, to include an engraved portrait on the title page of the First Folio edition of Shakespeare's collected plays, published in 1623 (FIG. 17). This image may have been in the process of being designed and engraved quite close in time to the construction of the Stratford bust, perhaps as little as a year or so later. But in addition to the different physical medium used in the First Folio – flat black-and-white engraving, rather than three-dimensional coloured stone sculpture – there are other major differences. There is also a question mark over the identity of the engraver, and the mystery of what sketch, portrait or miniature the engraving could have been based on. It was undoubtedly the inspiration for the best and most pleasing of the many 'fake' portraits of Shakespeare.

While the Stratford bust was apparently designed to show the poet as a mature man, at the summit of his lifetime fame, the so-called Droeshout engraving depicts him as a considerably younger man, possibly as he appeared around 1599–1602, at the

17 (*previous spread*)
Title page of the First Folio.

peak of his Elizabethan success. This is appropriate, since about half of the thirty-six plays included in the First Folio appear to have been written during the reign of Elizabeth I, who died in March 1603. The poet looks slimmer, as well as younger, in the Droeshout engraving than he does in the Stratford bust. His hair already recedes from a dome-like brow, but it is more abundant, and appears darker, than in the bust. However, too much should not be made of precise hair colour since the Stratford bust was repeatedly 'restored' and repainted, as described in the previous chapter. In any case, an engraving, printed in black on white, does not enable the craftsman to indicate clearly whether the subject's hair was light brown, dark brown or almost black.

Portrait engravings were rarely original compositions. After the invention of printing, but before the invention of photography, engraving was the chief means by which multiple copies of an existing portrait could be produced and made widely available. It seems likely that Droeshout's engraving is modelled on a painting or sketch of Shakespeare made around 1600. It would be natural to link this apparently lost original to the line in a play of 1599–1600 already quoted in Chapter 1: 'O Sweet Master Shakespeare, I'll have his picture in my study at the court.' Though no early image has ever been convincingly identified, we cannot be sure that no such 'picture' ever existed.

Pictorial artefacts have a generic tendency to disappear if not very carefully preserved. This may be what happened to the earliest representations of Shakespeare. Also, if Droeshout is based on a sketch, it may not have been thought particularly important to preserve the original sketch once the engraving on which it was based had been made. Disposing of it would be analogous to the regular practice according to which a playwright's 'foul papers' were not preserved once a text had reached what was believed to be the permanence of print.

Also, there are two well-documented conflagrations in which an image or images of Shakespeare could plausibly have been destroyed. The first, which occurred within Shakespeare's lifetime, is the burning to the ground of the Globe Theatre on 29 July 1613, early during a performance of *Henry VIII*. To add extra power to this spectacular and often pageant-like play, real cannon-fire had been used in the key scene of a splendid feast and masque at Cardinal Wolsey's house, in which the king was to meet Anne Boleyn for the first time. In this performance, however, that momentous encounter was never enacted. The thatch of the playhouse was ignited by gunpowder, and within little more than an hour the whole playhouse was burnt to the ground. Mercifully, the theatre was evacuated very speedily, and there was no loss of life or major injury – just a pair of badly singed breeches.[1] It seems probable that the tower-like structure at the back of the stage known as the tiring house was used for the storage not only of costumes and props, but also of books, papers and other theatre-related items, and that those were all destroyed. This material may well have included portraits of some of the leading players. The second conflagration that might have led to the loss of a portrait or portraits of Shakespeare is the Great Fire of London of September 1666, which saw the destruction of a large part of the City. There may have been admirers of Shakespeare within the City of London whose chattels included Shakespearean memorabilia – books and pictures – and pictures of him may also have hung in some of the City's many taverns.

Lovers of Shakespeare's works, with very few exceptions, have been deeply disappointed by the Droeshout engraving. M.H. Spielmann speaks for many in his negative comments:

> The hair does not balance on the two sides; the ear is malformed; the cupid's bow of the mouth … is utterly contradictory of the mouth in the bust … the head is much too big for the body,

while the exaggerated and distorted perspective of the lines of
the dress, as well as of the trimming of it, especially on the left
(with the grotesquely large and vilely drawn 'shoulder-wings')
show that this portion at least was not done from life.[2]

The final observation here – that the upper body, clad in a but-
toned doublet, 'was not done from life' – is particularly telling.
The way in which the head, tightly encased in a starched collar,
appears to float free above the too-small doubleted body below
may tell us something about the method by which the image
was created. The face was almost certainly modelled on an image
originally drawn from life, c.1600. The doublet, however, could
belong to almost anyone of the status of a gentleman or above.[3]

If the original image on which Droeshout was based was a
rough sketch, rather than a fully finished portrait in oils, that
might account for the curious blankness of both the domed brow
and the smooth cheeks. The latter especially seem like Empty
Quarters, and leave us with no strong sense of the poet's features
or expression beyond the fact that he had been freshly barbered,
judging by the short bristles or shading on the chin and lower
cheeks. Another possibility is that Droeshout is based on a portrait
miniature; in these the practice was not to add or even suggest
any shading. My own suspicion is that the image that has reached
us has been rather clumsily – perhaps hastily – put together by
combining a sketch of Shakespeare's face made when he was in his
thirties with a randomly chosen model for a gentlemanly doublet
that was designed and engraved by another hand.

Early printing practices

During the Elizabethan to Jacobean period the preliminary material in a book was normally the last collection of copy to be
delivered to the printers in order to be set up in print. This

material included the book's dedication – in this instance, the dedication made by Heminges and Condell to the munificent earls of Pembroke and Montgomery – along with other prefatory matter including an author portrait and various commendatory verses. As several recent studies have shown, the making of the First Folio was a costly and time-consuming project. It is highly likely that by October 1622, when the book was advertised in the English edition of the Frankfurt Book Fair catalogue, it was running both over time and over budget, to use a phrase familiar in our own age. The First Folio seems not to have been on sale until the winter of 1623.[4] That may explain why the title-page image is so crude, even clumsy. The engraver, or engravers, may have been under great pressure to produce the illustration speedily, to avoid causing yet more delay. This perhaps led to its being prepared by more than one engraver – an experienced craftsman for the head, and an apprentice or much less experienced colleague

To the Reader.

This Figure, that thou here feeſt put,
    It was for gentle Shakeſpeare cut;
Wherein the Grauer had a ſtrife
    with Nature, to out-doo the life :
O, could he but haue drawne his wit
    As well in braſſe, as he hath hit
His face ; the Print would then ſurpaſſe
    All, that vvas euer vvrit in braſſe.
But, ſince he cannot, Reader, looke
    Not on his Picture, but his Booke.
                                         B. I.

18 Verses by Ben Jonson opposite the title page of the First Folio.

for the body. Some unfortunate miscalculation led to a noticeable mismatch between the large head and the too-small body over which it is positioned. It is likely that neither the time available nor the (small) size of the agreed fee permitted any remedial work.

The short poem by Ben Jonson on the facing page (FIG. 18) seems to reflect such a scenario. It may have come as an unpleasant shock to Jonson to encounter at a very late stage of the printers' work such a vacuous and clumsy representation of his friend and fellow playwright. He seems to anticipate that contemporary admirers of Shakespeare's plays in 1623 will also be shocked:

To the Reader.

This Figure, that thou here seest put,
  It was for gentle Shakespeare cut;
Wherein the Graver had a strife
  with Nature, to out-doo the life:
O, could he but have drawne his wit
  As well in brasse, as he hath hit
His face; the Print would then surpasse
  All, that was ever writ in brasse.
But, since he cannot, Reader, looke
  Not on his Picture, but his Booke.

The first few lines may be read as suggesting sarcastically that the likeness is so poor that fans of Shakespeare's plays – some of whom may have been familiar with his appearance, both on stage and off – had to have it explained to them that, though it was intended to represent 'gentle Shakespeare', it did so very inadequately. It may also suggest, satirically, that in the 'strife' or competition between 'the Graver' and 'Nature', Nature was the clear winner. Had the engraved portrait lived up to the brilliance of the dead poet's wit, that would be wonderful, but it does not. The best thing for the reader to do is to turn the page as quickly as possible before plunging with enjoyment into the plays.

Who was ultimately responsible for the manufacture of this inadequate portrait? It bears the inscription, bottom left, *Martin Droeshout sculpsit London[iensi]. –* that is, 'Martin Droeshout engraved [it] in London'. The first question, however, is which Martin Droeshout was laying claim to the work. There has been a long tradition of attributing it to the Martin Droeshout who was a grandson of John Droeshout, a joiner and painter who came from Brussels to London in 1566. His elder son, Michael, was an engraver rather than a painter, and it has long been believed that the man responsible for the First Folio portrait was Michael's son Martin – both father and son being, allegedly, 'second-rate craftsmen'.[5] For after-comers there was some comfort in this attribution, for the Martin Droeshout whose grandfather was John was barely 22 at the time when the First Folio portrait was engraved, and possibly still an apprentice rather than a fully qualified master craftsman. However, there has been much puzzlement about why such a major task should have been assigned to an inexperienced engraver.

Which Martin Droeshout?

It has recently been argued that the 22-year-old Martin Droeshout was almost certainly not the engraver of the First Folio portrait. It is not even certain that he worked as an engraver.[6] A case has been made for the craftsman in question being a much older man, the namesake and uncle of the younger Martin Droeshout. The senior Martin Droeshout, a freeman of the Painter-Stainers' Company – there was no professional association of engravers at the time – had been born in Brussels in the 1560s. Latterly he resided in the parish of St Olave's, Hart Street, in the City of London, very close to the residence of John Heminges. Far from being young and inexperienced, this man was in his late fifties, possibly even over

Martin D. sc.   James Marquis of Hamilton.&c.   London 1623.

60 – a considerable age for the time. But this radically different attribution introduces further problems. There is a substantial body of engravings attributed in inscriptions to MD, or bearing a monogram of *M.DR* or *M.Droeshout*. Many of these attributions are, as in the case of the First Folio of Shakespeare, included in books of considerable stature, and some are portraits.

There is a particularly startling contrast between Droeshout's portrait of Shakespeare and another that was apparently completed by the same craftsman in the very same year, 1623. This one depicts James, 2nd marquess of Hamilton (1589–1625), a close friend and favourite of King James I. This too bears a small inscription beneath: *Martin D. sc.[7] London, 1623* (FIG. 19). This is evidently based on a grand full-length portrait which showed its noble subject standing, in half-armour and splendid breeches, with a large plumed helmet resting on a table to the subject's left. The contrast between this splendid and beautifully detailed engraving and the almost embarrassingly crude and inadequate portrait of Shakespeare, apparently fashioned by the same craftsman in the same year, could hardly be more striking. The likely explanation, however, is simple.

As already mentioned, in a period that long pre-dated the invention of photography, engraving provided the normal means by which images were copied and reproduced. The chief reason why the engraved portrait of the marquess of Hamilton is so good, and the engraved portrait of Shakespeare so bad, is probably attributable to major differences between the character and quality of the originals on which the engravings were based. The image of the marquess was evidently based on a splendid full-length oil painting of a major aristocrat and royal favourite. In contrast, the Shakespeare portrait seems to have been based either on a poor sketch or on a limning in miniature that lacked shading.

There may also be external reasons for the huge divergence in quality between these two images. As already suggested, the

19 Portrait engraving of James, 2nd marquess of Hamilton, made by M. Droeshout in 1623.

budget for the production of the great First Folio was probably beginning to be stretched beyond its limits by the time the portrait was commissioned. There was considerable pressure to complete the printing work so that the editors and publishers could at last begin to garner some financial recompense for their substantial investment. Droeshout's commission to engrave Hamilton's portrait surely commanded a large fee since the work was highly detailed and must have taken some time. The Hamilton project was also of an entirely different kind, this being a free-standing portrait engraving to be displayed as a picture by his friends and relations, rather than an author-portrait, contemplation of which, as Jonson made clear in his verses, should not detain the reader for very long, since the book's real interest lay in all those plays. But, as we shall see, despite Droeshout being widely regarded as unattractive, the medium in which it was created led to its being very frequently reproduced or copied, both in later editions of the First Folio and elsewhere.

The Droeshout engraving became if possible even less attractive in later editions. Some small alterations to the plate were made for the frontispiece of the Second Folio (1632) – such as an extra line of hair on the right. By 1685, when the Fourth Folio was being prepared, the engraved plate appears to have been much worn as a result of frequent reprintings of large print runs. The image was subjected to 'Violent cross-hatching over nearly the whole plate: forehead, nose, lips, moustache, cheeks, and chin, and hair... All is vigorously seared across in various directions in the vain hope of bringing back force and life into the worn used up plate.'[8]

There is a striking parallel here to the unhappy story of the Stratford bust. In both cases, Shakespeare's still burgeoning fame led to physical restoration of his image being undertaken which was essentially damaging, rendering an already somewhat crude image even less satisfactory.

Later versions and a fake?

Rather more successful, aesthetically at least, were some seventeenth-century engravings based on Droeshout. For instance, a collection of Shakespeare's *Poems* printed in 1640 carries a frontispiece freshly engraved by William Marshall (FIG. 20). It

This Shadowe is renowned Shakespear's? Soule of th'age
The applause? delight? the wonder of the Stage.
Nature her selfe, was proud of his designes
And joy'd to weare the dressing of his lines;
The learned will Confess, his works are such,
As neither man, nor Muse, can prayse to much.
For ever live thy fame, the world to tell;
Thy like, no age, shall ever paralell.

20 Portrait engraving based on Droeshout, made by William Marshall as the frontispiece to Shakespeare's *Poems* (1640). Bodleian Library, Arch. G f.4.

is based on a reversed image of Droeshout, and shows the poet with what appears to be a halo of light behind him. He wears a cloak loosely draped over his right shoulder, while in his right hand, elegantly gloved, he holds a sprig of bay, the symbol of poetic inspiration. As a half-length image contained within an oval frame, this is considerably more attractive than Droeshout. Whether it is better or worse as a likeness of Shakespeare when alive we have no way of judging.

More quirkily, a small image of Shakespeare's head within an oval frame – engraved by William Faithorne, and apparently based on Marshall's portrait – appears as a frontispiece to John Quarles's adaptation and extension of Shakespeare's narrative poem *The Rape of Lucrece*, published in 1594. Here, the framed portrait of Shakespeare, with a disconcertingly smug smile, appears to float free above Faithorne's image of the rapist Tarquin. The rapist is gazing in wonder at his victim, who is in the process of stabbing herself with a rather large and heavy-looking sword. To modern eyes this composition looks rather repellent in seeming to present a Shakespeare who is particularly proud of his ability to describe rape and self-slaughter (FIG. 21).

There is another treatment of the Droeshout engraving that continues to enjoy some prominence and status, even though it is, strictly speaking, a fake. This is the painting known as the Flower portrait that is now in the possession of the Royal Shakespeare Company in Stratford-upon-Avon (FIG. 22). It is closely based on the portrait in the First Folio, but is an oil painting and quite effectively coloured. For instance, Shakespeare's starched stand-up ruff may be seen to be translucent. The doublet's frogging and buttons are quite delicately painted to give an effect of gold, not overdone. The subject's hair and beard tend towards a gingery-brown colour. The painting bears an inscription, also apparently in gold, *Willm Shakespeare, 1609*. However, the picture's provenance

The Fates decree, that 'tis a mighty wrong
To Woemen Kinde, to have more Greife, then Tongue

21 Image of Shakespeare based on Droeshout in William Faithorne engraving on the title page to John Quarles's adaptation of *The Rape of Lucrece* (1655). Bodleian Library, Mal. 889.

and history cannot be traced before it came into the possession of a man called H.C. Clements, *c.*1840. It was purchased by Edgar Flower from Clements's estate in 1892. The Royal Shakespeare Company already possessed a few Shakespeare-related paintings. In 1895 Flower donated this apparent gem to the company for their collection.

There were many viewers who believed Flower to be a genuine seventeenth-century artefact, and it must have given some pleasure, as a rather more pleasing version of Stratford's Swan of Avon than the Droeshout engraving with which it is so evidently connected. However, most modern art historians have had grave doubts about the painting's authenticity. Doubts at last gave way to certainties in 2005, when 'Following detailed technical examination at the National Portrait Gallery ... it was categorically identified as a product of the early nineteenth century.'[9]

22 The Flower portrait of Shakespeare, *c.1820–40.*

Underneath the upper layers of paint a damaged, though genuine, Italian painting of the Madonna and Child from the mid-1500s became visible. Elizabethan and Jacobean painters did occasionally reuse old paintings done on panel for secular portraits, partly because panel itself was an expensive item. However, clinching proof that this was not what happened in the case of the Flower portrait emerged with the discovery, through chemical analysis, that a blue pigment used by the Flower painter was the synthetic French ultramarine, which was not available until 1828.[10] The current consensus is that the portrait is the work of an artist of the mid-nineteenth century – unknown, though evidently quite skilful.

Modern versions

Because of its technical simplicity as a rather crude black-and-white image, the Droeshout engraving has enjoyed, and still enjoys, a vigorous afterlife. Charmless though it may be, it is far and away the most immediately recognizable image of Shakespeare, as well as the easiest to reproduce. This has led to its frequent inclusion on theatre programmes, on greetings cards and party invitations, in advertising, on dustjackets and in many other visual manifestations.

23 (*below, left*) Amalgamated image of Droeshout with Chandos used to advertise Cigar Lights (*c.* 1880). Bodleian Library, John Johnson Collection, Labels 12 (43c).

24 (*below, right*) Shakespeare seeking inspiration in tea (*c.* 1930). Bodleian Library, John Johnson Collection, Tea and Coffee 1 (72d).

A late-nineteenth-century example that demonstrates the usefulness of Droeshout is a crude image of Shakespeare used to advertise Cigar Lights, preserved in the Bodleian Library's John Johnson Collection of printed ephemera (FIG. 23). There are many other examples of Shakespeare's image being used to sell commodities, including a lively image showing Shakespeare, desperate for inspiration, being wonderfully perked up by 'tea tips' (FIG. 24). Much more recent is the version of Droeshout that appears as the book jacket of Laurie Maguire and Emma Smith's *30 Great Myths about Shakespeare* (2012). Droeshout has been washed in DayGlo™

colours, the poet's blue face and scarlet collar clashing violently with a shocking pink background. Even the dull black hair of the original engraving has been lightened up with some orangey-gold highlights (FIG. 25).

More than the Stratford bust or the so-called Chandos portrait, Droeshout, in its black-and-white clarity of outline, provides an immediately recognizable icon representing Shakespeare – familiar even to people who have never read a line of Shakespeare's writings.

25 Droeshout image of Shakespeare brightly recoloured for the jacket of Laurie Maguire and Emma Smith's book *30 Great Myths about Shakespeare* (Wiley-Blackwell, 2012).

FOUR

The Chandos portrait

DOZENS OF PORTRAITS have been claimed as likenesses of Shakespeare done from life, but only one holds its own. This is the so-called Chandos portrait. It is widely accepted as genuine because of an apparently continuous chain of documented evidence, resulting in a provenance leading from its creator and original owner to the theatre manager Sir William Davenant and beyond. It is unique among painted images apparently of Shakespeare, both in its documentation and in the freshness of its treatment of the sitter. The latter has suggested to many viewers that it must have been painted from life. However, many of this chain's links are accompanied by uncertainties. The first of these is the previously unresolved identity of the 'Jo: Taylor' who was allegedly the portrait's creator and earliest owner. Working backwards from the early eighteenth century, it is possible to re-examine parts of the chain and arrive at a new case for the identity of the painter and the nature of his friendship with Shakespeare (FIG. 26).

My first witness is the prolific engraver, painter and art historian George Vertue (1684–1756), who was, in addition to many other interests, a Shakespeare enthusiast. The earliest of his many copiously inscribed notebooks, assembled between 1713 and 1721, is British Library MS Add. 21,111. Describing its contents as 'these Historys of Collections', Vertue assembled data about

26 (*previous spread*)
The Chandos portrait
of Shakespeare.

Car.

G Vertue
1741

painters, paintings, patrons and much else, in the form of randomly accumulated notes to be written up and ordered at a later date.[1] Shakespeare makes half a dozen appearances, three of which throw considerable light on the origins of the Chandos portrait.

Vertue's admiration for Shakespeare is visually expressed in a carefully penned self-portrait fronting the notebook (FIG. 27). A splendidly jacketed and bewigged Vertue sits at his desk, turning his face to confront the spectator while pointing with his right index figure at his own portrait engraving of Shakespeare. Though tiny, it is clear that this image is based on what is nowadays called the Chandos portrait. From 1710 until 1719, the Chandos portrait was in the possession of Robert Keck, a lawyer and art collector who had fine lodgings in the Inner Temple. In the notebook's frontispiece Vertue's studio is shown as crammed with objects, including a bust of Charles I perched on top of a high wooden case; a miniature of Charles II; a painter's palette; and brushes, colours and a couple of apparently unfinished miniatures. Amid the clutter, the viewer's eye is drawn from Vertue's full-frontal gaze down his right shoulder, arm and hand, leading to his pointing forefinger and the image to which it is directed: a painted or engraved miniature of the Chandos portrait. Vertue seems almost to touch Shakespeare's left eye with his fingertip. Not only does he honour Shakespeare in this gesture; he implicitly identifies the Chandos image of Shakespeare as the best, superior both to the memorial bust in Holy Trinity Church, Stratford-upon-Avon, and to the Droeshout engraving that fronts the 1623 First Folio edition of Shakespeare's plays.

It is striking that Chandos was also chosen by Nicholas Rowe as the basis of the handsomely elaborated portrait engraving by Michael van der Gucht that fronts his 1709 edition of Shakespeare's plays (FIG. 28). As Michael Caines has recently shown, this was an elegant and costly publication with 'high production values'.[2] Though not always to be trusted on the topic of Shakespeare's

27 Self-portrait by George Vertue. London, British Library, MS ADD 21,111, frontispiece.

M.V. Gucht Sculp:

W O

Mr Will

SIX

ADORN

Revis'd and Corr
the Life and W
By N.

LO
Printe for Jacob
Gate next Grave

biography, Rowe, himself a London playwright, was well placed to form a judgement on the authenticity of Chandos.

Vertue's notes are untidy, and much corrected and recorrected. They are not always easy to read, and evidently not always reliable since in the course of revisiting notes he often alters previous jottings. In doing so, however, Vertue was aiming at accuracy. His tendency to revise and correct is especially notice-able in passages in which he discusses portraits of Shakespeare. In the first of these, Vertue alludes to 'the Picture of Shaksper painted & in possession of the Lord Halifax' – a note which he later corrected by describing it as 'a copy'. It is also described as a painting made by Sir Godfrey Kneller for the poet Dryden, so there is no question of this item being a Jacobean painting, still less an *ad vivum* image of the subject.

The next Shakespeare allusion is much more interesting. I quote it in full, expanding contracted words and letters:

> The Picture of Shakespeare the only one Original in Possession of M*aste*r Keyck of the Temple. he boughte for forty guines of M*aste*r Baterton who bought it of *Sir Willia*m Davenant \to whom it/ who had it of Shakespear. it was painted by one Taylor a Player contemp*orary* with Shake*speare* and his intimate Friend.

At a later date Vertue made two additions, both of which he subsequently deleted. In the left-hand margin, alongside the allu-sion to 'Baterton' – that is, the great Restoration actor Thomas Betterton (1635–1710) – he has neatly written the name Richard Burbridge, but has then firmly crossed this out. Something similar has happened in the case of the words 'a Player'. He has written above, in rather small letters, '& painter' – only to cross that out. On second and third thoughts, therefore, presumably in response to an informant whose testimony Vertue had come to regard as untrustworthy, he firmly deleted both of the additions.

28 Engraved portrait based on Chandos by Michael van der Gucht in volume I of Nicholas Rowe's edition of Shakespeare's *Plays* (1709). Bodleian Library, Mal. C 83.

Strangely, Vertue's repeated scoring out of the words '& painter' has been ignored by modern scholars. They have invoked the description as evidence that whoever painted the portrait in question must have been a painter, as well as – or perhaps rather than – a player. In her very informative essay on the Chandos portrait in the book that accompanied the National Portrait Gallery's excellent *Searching for Shakespeare* exhibition in 2006, Dr Tarnya Cooper does not question the widespread assumption that the Chandos artist must have been a painter by profession – possibly the John Taylor who was discovered by the late Mary Edmond to have been a master painter-stainer from 1626 to 1648. This is odd, given that in Vertue's two most substantial notes on the Chandos portrait, both of them reproduced in the *Searching for Shakespeare* catalogue, he has allowed the words 'a Player' to stand, while the words 'a painter' have been crossed out. Though it may seem natural to suspect the creator of a painting of being 'a painter', this appears not to be the case here.

Vertue's next substantial allusion to the portrait under discussion strengthens previous testimony that the creator of Chandos was a player, not a painter:

> Master Betterton told Master Keck several times that the picture of Shakespeare he had, was painted by one John Taylor. a Player who acted for Shakespear & this John Taylor in his will left it to Sir William Davenant. Master Betterton boughte it, & at his death Master Keck bought it. in whos Possesion it now is.

The surname Taylor was, and still is, very common – almost as common as Jones or Smith. The Christian name John was if anything even more common. Although a painter-stainer called John Taylor has been identified, his dates are too late for him to have painted Shakespeare from life, and his will includes no bequest to William Davenant.

I suggest that during the passage of these anecdotes through various intermediaries before they reached George Vertue, someone misread or misconstrued the name of the individual who painted Shakespeare's portrait from life. In sixteenth- and seventeenth-century documents, Christian names, especially common ones, are frequently abbreviated to two initial letters, leaving scope for subsequent confusion. Edmund Spenser, for instance, liked to sign himself Ed. Sp., the first word of which could hypothetically be read in later years as standing for Edward rather than Edmund. The two-letter abbreviation Jo: would normally be understood as representing the very popular Christian name John, rather than the relatively uncommon Joseph. According to E.G. Withycombe's excellent *Oxford Dictionary of English Christian Names* (1977), 15 per cent of boys born in England between 1550 and 1599 were christened John. The name's popularity was to burgeon further. Between 1600 and 1649 the proportion of Johns rose to 19 per cent of christened males, and between 1650 and 1699 it rose yet further, to 28 per cent. By the end of the seventeenth century, therefore, nearly a third of males born in England after 1650 were called John. It would not be at all surprising therefore if a late-seventeenth- or early-eighteenth-century witness simply assumed that a name recorded as 'Jo Taylor' alluded to a man whose first name was John.

'A player who acted for Shakespeare'

There is an alternative, which may be seen as a useful application of the *lectio difficilior* principle. In the course of multiple transcriptions of texts, an unusual word — or, in this case, an unusual proper name — will tend to be replaced with a more familiar one. According to Miss Withycombe, the name Joseph was 'Not widely used until the seventeenth century'. Also, 'many of the medieval *Josephs* were Jews', and there was no feast day in England dedicated to St Joseph until 1624. Nevertheless, the name was reasonably familiar to Elizabethan and Jacobean godparents. The actors recorded in the 1623 First Folio list as having performed in Shakespeare's plays include a young man called Joseph Taylor. He rose to prominence in or before 1610, and continued to perform an interestingly varied range of leading roles until the ban on the public performance of plays in 1642. This man, who was eventually to become Burbage's successor, may have resembled Burbage in being an outstanding player who was also a fine amateur painter. This was the view of Edmond Malone, the great eighteenth-century Shakespeare scholar. According to Andrew Gurr, who wrote the entry on Malone for the *Oxford Dictionary of National Biography* in 2006, 'On some evidence that has not survived, Edmond Malone thought that [Joseph Taylor] might have painted the Chandos portrait of Shakespeare.'

If we explore the possibility that the man called Taylor who was both 'a player' and Shakespeare's 'intimate Friend' bore the relatively unusual name of Joseph, rather than the very common name John, some other details fall into place. The player Joseph Taylor (1586–1652) is not obscure. His entry in the *Oxford Dictionary of National Biography* was prepared by Andrew Gurr, assisted by the late Mary Edmond. Apparently christened on 6 February 1586 in the London parish of St Andrew by the Wardrobe, Joseph Taylor first appears in documentary records as a player in 1610, as one of seven men who led the company called the Duke of York's Men. He may have belonged to it from its creation in 1608. Their royal patron was the 8-year-old Prince Charles, James I's frail younger son, future king and martyr. In 1610, aged 23 to 24, Joseph Taylor was one of the younger members of the duke's company. He quickly made his mark as an outstanding performer, and in 1611 became the leading member of the next newly formed royal playing company, that of the Lady Elizabeth's Men.

The First Folio's list of actors who appeared 'in all these plays' indicates that Joseph Taylor 'acted for Shakespeare' in the broad sense that he acted in plays written by Shakespeare. I believe that he may have done so within Shakespeare's lifetime. Vertue's notes also suggest that there was more to their relationship than that – Taylor became the older man's 'intimate Friend'. A further witness supports Vertue's claim, though this has been widely dismissed. In his *Roscius Anglicanus* (1708) John Downes records that William Davenant described 'Master *Taylor* of the Black Fryars' as having played the part of Hamlet:

> The Tragedy of *Hamlet*: *Hamlet* being performed by Master Betterton, Sir William [Davenant] (having seen Master *Taylor* of the Black Fryars Company Act it, who being instructed by the Author Master Shakspear) taught Master Betterton in every particle of it.

Thorough instruction of a charismatic young player by a brilliant older one might easily lead to the younger man becoming the older man's 'intimate Friend'. The dates seem to fit. Joseph Taylor, described by Vertue as having 'acted for Shakespeare', may have done so in more than one sense. Early in his career, it seems, he was selected to perform the most celebrated and surely also most challenging Shakespearean role, that of Hamlet, being meticulously coached for it by Shakespeare himself. This enabled Davenant, in turn, to mimic Taylor's treatment of the role for the benefit of Betterton, while Betterton, whose most prized role this was, faithfully mimicked Davenant's instructions. He continued to perform the role of Hamlet when he was over 70.

Shakespeare's tuition of Joseph Taylor may have taken place either in 1610, when Taylor first rose to prominence as a member of a royally sponsored playing company, or a year or two later, after he had become the leading member of Lady Elizabeth's Men. Such a promotion suggests conspicuous ability. By 1610/11 Taylor was undoubtedly acquainted with John Heminges, from whom he acquired some King's Men's costumes for his new company. Given the well-documented closeness between Heminges and Shakespeare, it may have been around this time that young Joseph Taylor became Shakespeare's 'intimate Friend'. He may have been under consideration as a possible successor to Burbage, now in his mid-forties, perhaps becoming rather old to be imagined as an undergraduate still receiving advice from his mother. In 1610/11 or later, Taylor may have painted the great playwright's portrait, retaining the picture as his own precious memento. As a private, personal image it shows the sitter in a relaxed, off-stage mood, with his white shirt collar unfastened. It is a pleasing paradox that such an informal artefact was eventually to find its way to a major public collection.

Those who believe that boundaries between playing companies were strictly observed may prefer to consider the possibility that Shakespeare's tuition of Joseph Taylor took place in or after the late summer of 1613, following the burning down of the Globe and Shakespeare's sale of his share in the King's Men. It is certainly plausible that *Hamlet*, a celebrated text to which Shakespeare surely had every right, was given fresh life by being performed by a different company, with a new and much younger Prince of Denmark.

Joseph Taylor quickly made his mark as an outstanding young performer. Telling testimony occurs in Jonson's carnivalesque comedy *Bartholomew Fair* (1614). In it the prodigal young squire Bartholomew Cokes 'of Harrow' interrogates Master Sharkwell, one of two theatrical doorkeepers, about the fair's forthcoming 'motion' – that is, puppet show – to help him to decide whether it will be worth his while to pay the large fee of 12 pence to view it. Cokes asks: 'What kind of *Actors* ha' you? Are they good *Actors*?' (5.3.118). When he discovers that the actors are merely puppets, whose tiring room – that is, dressing room – is a humble basket, Cokes pours scorn on this troupe in comparison with the brilliant living performers who are to be viewed on the stage proper: 'I thinke, one *Taylor*, would goe neere to beat all this company, with a hand bound behind him … which is your *Burbage* now? … Your best *Actor*. Your *Field*?'

The allusions appear to be to three outstanding actors of the day, Joseph Taylor, Richard Burbage and Nathan Field. Cokes names Taylor first, seeing him as an exceptionally brilliant young player who could, to use a still-current idiom, steal the show even 'with his hands tied behind his back'. It may be a token of the extent to which modern stage historians have overlooked the star status of Joseph Taylor that, in the text of *Bartholomew Fair* in the new Cambridge Jonson (2012), Taylor's name has been reduced to lower case and 'regularized' to Tailor, with an explanatory note speculatively associating the passage with disparaging proverbs about professional tailors. This reading does not make sense, since it is clear in context that all three actors are invoked by Cokes as outstanding performers, with Taylor as the star that currently shines most brightly in the Jacobean theatrical firmament. All three players are praised, not mocked. Their names are invoked to underline the inevitable inferiority of the non-human actors at the fair, who are about to perform a rather old-fashioned play about Hero and Leander. The passage also incorporates an in-joke, since all three named actors appeared in the play's two documented performances. The first was at the Hope Theatre on 31 October 1614; the second, the following night, for the court at Whitehall, in the presence of King James.

London or Stratford?

When, and in what context, might Joseph Taylor have painted a portrait of Shakespeare? According to the earliest accounts of Shakespeare's life, these men had little opportunity to meet, let alone to become close friends. In 1708 the affable but languid Nicholas Rowe – who did not visit Stratford-upon-Avon, and lived before the age of thorough archival research – sent many subsequent biographers along a purely speculative track in claiming that 'The latter part of his [Shakespeare's] life was spent, as all men of good sense will wish theirs may be, in ease, retirement and the conversation of his friends ... [he] is said to have spent some years before his death at his native Stratford.'

Rowe does not tell us who it was who 'said' this. Shakespeare certainly had good friends in and around Stratford – such as Thomas Russell, who was to be appointed overseer of his will – but that doesn't mean that he preferred their company to that of his theatrical colleagues. Overall, Rowe relied on a research trip to Stratford made by the elderly Betterton, which included some muddled scrutiny of the Holy Trinity parish registers. For instance, Betterton gave Shakespeare's father 'John' far too many children, confusing him with a Stratford namesake – an illustration of the frequent occurrence of the Christian name John. In any case, whoever it was who said that the latter part of Shakespeare's life was spent in Stratford, we now know that the claim was mistaken.

Thanks to the labours of modern scholars, we are aware of documents which testify to the continuance of Shakespeare's residence in London. The most substantial one is the record of his purchase, on 10 March 1613, of the capacious and splendid Blackfriars Gatehouse that had once been the Dominican Prior's lodging. A mediaeval historian has suggested to me that this was where Henry V had conferred with his Privy Council. Many traditionally minded biographers, over-influenced by Rowe's casual remark about Shakespeare's sensible 'retirement', have claimed that the Gatehouse was purely an investment property, rather than a purchase that enabled the poet to live in London in considerable style, while enjoying close proximity both to the King's Wardrobe and to the Blackfriars Theatre. The previous owner of the Gatehouse, Henry Walker, 'citizen and minstrel', may also have had connections with London's theatres.

Later and more probing studies of Shakespeare's life suggest that Rowe's idyll of Shakespeare's provincial retirement is a vacuous fancy. The large deed of conveyance relating to the Gatehouse survives in two copies. One, bearing Shakespeare's signature, is in London's Guildhall Library, while another is in the Folger Shakespeare Library in Washington DC. The Blackfriars purchase was made in legal partnership with Shakespeare's friend and colleague John Heminges, along with two other prominent Londoners, William Johnson, landlord of the celebrated Mermaid Tavern, and John Jackson, a wine trader of a literary bent. Made in association with such well-established and congenial Londoners, this complex transaction points to a decision on Shakespeare's part to involve himself more, not less, with the lively and diverse world of London theatres and London society. And, as has been pointed out by previous scholars, the method of purchase precluded Shakespeare's wife, should she outlive him, from making any claim on the London residence.

The Blackfriars purchase was a venture that Shakespeare had probably been contemplating for some time. It made his decision to withdraw from the Globe after it burnt to the ground on 29 June 1613 very straightforward; he sold his share in the King's Men, and did not contribute to the cost of rebuilding the Globe. His cultural centre of gravity had already shifted to the north bank of the Thames. That substantial new property sorted well with Shakespeare's still-rising status in the Jacobean court. The second decade of James's peaceful reign saw a proliferation of new companies sponsored by members of the royal family, as well as of elite indoor performances and performance spaces.

Shakespeare had every reason to find the London theatrical scene congenial and lively during what sadly proved to be the last two and a half years of his life. Though *The Tempest*, with its valedictory close, may well be the last play Shakespeare wrote alone, evidence for his continued collaboration with other playwrights, such as Fletcher and Middleton, accumulates almost by the month. *The Tempest* itself enjoyed what was surely a spectacular performance at court during the Christmas season of 1613. The play's conclusion in a royal marriage made it especially apt for the betrothal of Princess Elizabeth to the Elector Palatine. There seem to have been at least seven other court performances of plays by Shakespeare during that winter. This was hardly a season in which Shakespeare would have chosen to rusticate himself to Stratford.

There is, in any case, further evidence for Shakespeare's continued residence in London: the commission in 1614 from Francis Manners to design a tournament *impresa* and motto for the Accession Day Tilts, an annual celebration of the monarch's accession.

Other documents point towards Shakespeare's presence in London both in 1614 and in 1615, in the form of some almost illegible entries in the so-called diary of Shakespeare's former friend and lodger, the attorney Thomas Greene, who was at the time Stratford's town clerk. On 17 November 1614 Greene visited 'my Cosen Shakspear … in towne … to see him how he did' – which may mean 'to see how he was getting on in his large Blackfriars residence'. On 23 December 1614 Greene recorded that he had written a letter in his own hand to 'Cosen Shakespeare', again trying to persuade him to lend support to resistance to the threatened enclosures in Stratford. Cryptic though they are, these allusions suggest both that Shakespeare was resident in London, and that he was largely indifferent to local affairs in Stratford. More interesting, though impossible to date, is the implication by Heminges and Condell in their epistle prefacing the First Folio that Shakespeare himself had planned to gather and edit texts of his own plays, a task that would probably have required continued residence in London. Family troubles and the onset of the illness that led to his death may have prevented him from making much headway with this project.

A precious memento

Joseph Taylor's vividly informal portrait of Shakespeare was, I suggest, painted some time between 1610 and 1615, somewhere in London, and was cherished as a precious memento of the training sessions he had enjoyed with the great playwright. It was allegedly bequeathed to William Davenant, though I have not located Joseph Taylor's will. In the hope that some reader is more skilled than I am in tracking down Surrey wills made during the Interregnum, I mention that he was buried in Richmond on 4 November 1652. However he acquired it, it appears that Davenant was the portrait's next owner, to be followed by Betterton and, after a brief spell when it was in the possession of the actress Mrs Barry, Robert Keck, who obtained it by purchase. An additional reason for believing both that the painting was the work of Joseph Taylor, and that it is an authentic likeness, is that this was the view of the earliest major biographer of Shakespeare, Edmond Malone.[3]

The portrait has undergone much interference, because of accumulated layers of paint and dirt and zealous cleaning, the latter leaving much of the original paint, already thin, very thin indeed. It is painted on slightly coarse canvas, rather than on more costly planed and primed wood. The weave of the canvas is painfully visible in several areas, including Shakespeare's face. But the 'lead tin yellow' used for the subject's earring has worn well. Recent

X-ray examinations made at the National Portrait Gallery have confirmed that it is an original detail. Like the unfastened collar, it shows Shakespeare off duty, while also hinting at his more splendid appearance in public. The simple gold earring is one to which, on formal occasions, a bright dangling jewel could be attached.

29 (*left*) Shakespeare and others in praise of candles (1889). Bodleian Library, John Johnson Collection, Oil and Candles 1(57).

30 (*opposite, above*) A ghostly Shakespeare, modelled on Chandos, recommends Effervescent Potash (*c.*1885). Bodleian Library, John Johnson Collection, Patent medicines 1 (1b).

31 (*opposite, below*) Shakespeare endorses Pears' soap (1902). Bodleian Library, John Johnson Collection, Soap 7 (13a).

The image conveys a powerful sense of presence. Though enclosed within a fashionable 'feigned oval', the sitter is attractively relaxed, lacking the posed stiffness of some grander portraits of the period. His posture and expression may reflect the agreeable rapport that prevailed between the distinguished player-playwright and the multi-talented young player who had recently become his 'intimate Friend'. Since this seems originally to have been a private image, we should be especially pleased that it reached its perfect home as the founding artefact of the National Portrait Gallery in 1856. This generous and far-sighted donation was made by Francis Egerton, 1st earl of Ellesmere – a man who was liberal in every sense of that word. It would have been better, in my opinion, to identify the work as the 'Ellesmere portrait' instead of invoking its previous noble owner, the prodigal and bankrupt duke of Chandos. It would be better still to rechristen it the 'Joseph Taylor portrait'.

Though considerably more elegant and subtle than Droeshout, the Chandos portrait has been a gift to advertisers across a wide range of commodities. For instance, in an unusually ambitious engraving of 1889, a version of Chandos shows Shakespeare as pre-eminent in a group of five 'Great English Writers' who have discussed the merits of 'Candles' (FIG. 29). Hawking patent medicine to a gullible woman, a ghostly and distinctly sinister Shakespeare advises her physician to recommend the consumption of 'Effervescent Potash', which was almost certainly toxic (FIG. 30). A more wholesome image has Shakespeare enthusiastically recommending Pears' soap (FIG. 31).

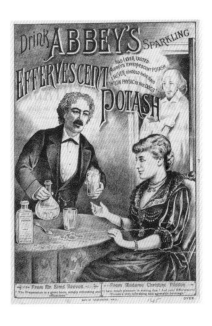

FIVE

Commemorative, disputed & other portraits

N INTERNATIONAL INDUSTRY that shows no sign of abating has now grown up around Shakespeare iconography. Other portraits of Shakespeare fall into two categories. The first is composed of images that make no claim to authenticity in terms of direct connection to Shakespeare when he was alive. These are essentially commemorative and celebratory. The second category is the large and ever expanding number of portraits for whose authenticity as images of Shakespeare claims have been made, honestly or otherwise. However we may feel about the artistic quality of each example, images included in the first category were generally well intentioned. Most of the representations discussed in this section may be aptly described as 'honourable' in intention, or even 'honorific' in so far as they were fashioned to do honour to Shakespeare's memory, and to keep it alive.

Commemorative portraits and sculptures

The great majority of the commemorative images are sculptures, but the very earliest example is a portrait. This is the fine painting of Shakespeare allegedly made by Gilbert Soest in about 1667 (FIG. 32). It is broadly based on the so-called 'Chandos' portrait, but is both more elegant and more detailed. The subject wears an

32 (*previous spread*)
Portrait of Shakespeare
attributed to Gilbert Soest,
c.1667.

elaborate doublet, resembling that in the Droeshout engraving, and his face and skin are rendered with subtle detail and colour. This was created as a memorial portrait, to provide Restoration playgoers with a pleasing image of Shakespeare. That is what it presumably did while in the possession of various collectors from about 1667 until 1959, when it was acquired by the Shakespeare Birthplace Trust.

The first and most splendid three-dimensional artefact in the commemorative category is the full-length marble sculpture carved by Peter Scheemakers in 1740/41 on the basis of a design by William Kent (FIG. 33). It was created for conspicuous display in Westminster Abbey's Poets' Corner. As Marcia Pointon has written,

> It combines the pointed beard and domed head of the effigy in Holy Trinity Church ... with the déshabillé relaxation of the Chandos portrait ... The effigy wears the eighteenth-century version of Van Dyck costume that was fashionable among the sitters of Reynolds and Gainsborough.[1]

This was an explicitly nationalistic creation. As Michael Dobson has shown, the construction and display of the image, in a prominent position in Poets' Corner, originally reflected a particular moment in British history: 'The bust of Shakespeare ... is the first monument to the playwright to celebrate him in a national context.'[2]

But, rather than celebrating the status quo in England, this statue was originally conceived as an embodiment of nationalist ideals that were 'specifically opposed by the government of the day'.[3] While other fictionalized images of Shakespeare have come and gone in popular favour, this one has endured. Some of its immediate applications were trivial, yet intimate. For instance, within a decade of its unveiling, the Kent/Scheemakers statue was 'reproduced in the form of a porcelain scent bottle'.[4] But it

33 Figure of Shakespeare carved by Scheemakers, in Poets' Corner, Westminster Abbey.

The Cloud capt Tow'rs
The Gorgeous Palaces
The Solemn Temples,
The Great Globe itself
Yea all which it Inherit,
Shall Dissolve
And like the baseless fabrick of a Vision
Leave not a wreck behind

GVL. KENT INV.   P. SCHEEMAKERS FT
                        MDCCXL

has also enjoyed more dignified forms of reproduction. In the 1980s, for instance, more than two and a half centuries on from its creation, the Poets' Corner image became familiar to everyone in Britain as an image of national status and quality when rather beautifully reproduced on the £20 banknote.

It is not surprising that this sculpture has long outlived its original political connotations, for it is a fine work of art, rightly admired by Westminster Abbey's many visitors. It does Shakespeare proud, supplying attractive features that are lacking from all three of the 'original' images. While the half-length bust in Holy Trinity Church, Stratford-upon-Avon, shows Shakespeare as at once podgy and rigid, Scheemakers's creation expresses a fluid torsion of the poet's body. He turns his head to the left as he rests his chin on his right fist; meanwhile his left arm curves gracefully down and to the poet's right, holding and pointing to a large unfolding piece of paper – much larger and grander than the simple sheet of paper that rests on a cushion in the Stratford image. Meanwhile, the lower half of his body – not indicated in any of the earlier images – suggests an almost balletic agility in the light crossing of the poet's right leg over the weight-bearing left, with his toes elegantly touching each other. This is a version of the then fashionable 'scissor-leg' pose. Scheemakers has also greatly improved the appearance of Shakespeare's hair. It is neither stiff and solid-seeming, as in Droeshout, nor casual and shaggy, as in Chandos – at least in the state in which Chandos has reached us. The sculptor is faithful to tradition in giving Shakespeare a receding hairline, but the waviness of his hair, full moustache and beard are attractively rendered, giving the poet a distinctly Cavalier look. Though there is no reason to believe that Shakespeare looked much like this, the Scheemakers image honours him in showing him as handsome and elegant – and perhaps a good dancer.

Many other honorific images have succeeded the Kent/
Scheemakers sculpture. Most of these have taken elements of
their design from one, two or all three of the primary images
discussed in Chapters 2–4. However, the next full-length sculpture of note (FIG. 34), while elegant and expressive in itself,
bears only a loose resemblance to earlier images of Shakespeare.
The celebrated actor David Garrick was the first, most famous

34 Figure of Shakespeare
sculpted by Louis-François
Roubiliac.

and perhaps most shamelessly egotistical, of various male actors who have performed major roles in Shakespeare's plays while also identifying themselves closely with Shakespeare the man. In 1756, having become extremely rich, Garrick sought to upstage the Scheemakers statue in Westminster Abbey with a splendid piece of work created by the great French sculptor Louis-François Roubiliac. Garrick himself posed as Shakespeare, and lent the subject a strong resemblance to himself, with smallish stature and a plump belly. As Michael Dobson remarks, 'The king of English literature is replaced even in effigy by the pre-eminent middle-class imposter.'[5]

This relaxed, unashamedly actorly image was originally designed for display in an octagonal temple in the grounds of Garrick's large house in Hampton-on-Thames. The childless Garrick bequeathed it to the British Museum, which of course bestowed an implicit National Monument status on it that strictly speaking it does not quite merit. However, its location ensures that it can be readily viewed by visitors to London, nowadays in the British Library rather than the British Museum. There is a smaller replica in the exclusive Garrick Club.

Many other honorific images have followed, both in Britain and worldwide. Most have taken elements of their design from one or more of the three primary images, not always with complete success. For instance, in 1911 a sculptor called Henry McCarthy created a recumbent image of Shakespeare, set within a wall-mounted frame, for Southwark Cathedral, in Shakespeare's time the large church known as St Mary Overie. It was designed to place Shakespeare in the company of other distinguished Southwark figures, most notably the fourteenth-century poet John Gower, whose nearby monument is detailed and brightly coloured. The Shakespeare effigy lies in front of a low-relief carved frieze of Southwark that shows places well known to Shakespeare, such as the Globe Theatre and London Bridge. These draw attention to Shakespeare's association with Southwark during most of his active career as an actor and playwright. But this recumbent Shakespeare looks strangely thin, and wears very brief round breeches that might look better on an Elizabethan teenager. The most unfortunate feature is the poet's head, modelled on Droeshout, which he rests on his left elbow in a posture that makes it look rather like a rugby ball. Nikolaus Pevsner, in his characteristically dry style, describes this effigy as 'a reclining figure in gelatinous brown alabaster'.

Shakespeare abroad

The Southwark monument was generously funded by an American philanthropist, Mr Sanford Saltus. Meanwhile, many other large and expensive images of Shakespeare had been created in the United States. For instance, New York's Central Park had a statue of Shakespeare as early as 1870, sculpted by John Quincy Adams Ward. Two of the many great US libraries, both on Capitol Hill, also have fine images of Shakespeare. One is in the Library of Congress, and was sculpted in bronze in 1896 by Frederick W. MacMonnies, whose style and technique were influenced by the years he spent in the École des Beaux-Arts in Paris in the 1880s (FIG. 35). His statue is a splendid, rather flamboyant creation that shows the poet in a confident upright pose, holding a large notebook in his left hand and a pen in his right. Toes turned out, he wears soft slippers which are adorned with supersized 'roses'. Taking a quite different and less fanciful approach, the Reading Room of the Folger Shakespeare Library is presided over by an excellent replica of the Stratford bust, which is better coloured and in every way far more attractive than the original bust in Holy Trinity, Stratford.

35 Statue of Shakespeare by
F.W. MacMonnies.

By the early to mid-twentieth century statues of Shakespeare adorned public spaces in many cities worldwide, such as Weimar in Germany, Elsinore in Denmark and Sydney in Australia – to name but three. This list is very far from comprehensive, but may suffice to show that a general desire to have a visual image of Shakespeare to contemplate – whether authentic or otherwise – has continued to develop side by side with admiration of his plays, whether read or performed. By this period he had become, to use the now currently fashionable term, iconic – and so he continues.

Other 'discoveries'

One early example of a 'new' Shakespeare portrait has already been discussed – the so-called 'Flower portrait', widely accepted as authentic until scientific analysis established its status as a mid-nineteenth-century forgery – based on Droeshout, but much prettier. To date, there have been at least sixty fake Shakespeare portraits, many of them believed at some time to be authentic before being proved otherwise.

Unlike the Flower portrait, the most interesting 'discoveries' of Shakespeare portraits have involved genuine Elizabethan and Jacobean works. None may be securely validated as an image of Shakespeare. As already mentioned, a seventeenth- or eighteenth-century owner of a genuine portrait of Shakespeare would surely have been proud of such a possession, even if it was not of high artistic quality. We would expect either an early inscription or a strong and continuous oral tradition going back to the seventeenth century, or both, to accompany and validate such an artefact. It would also be included in household inventories. But no such image has been traced to Stratford-upon-Avon or its environs.

In the early twentieth century claims were made for two genuine Elizabethan portraits of young men as images of Shakespeare. The first to surface as a contender was the one known as the Sanders portrait (FIG. 36), the ownership of which may be traced back to a John Sanders, who died in 1882. It was brought to public notice as a portrait of Shakespeare in the early 1900s. The evidence for the sitter's identity takes the form of a damaged paper label, which has become even more damaged since it was first examined, attached to the back of the painting. It apparently bore this description: 'Shakpere / Born April 23 =1564 / Died April 23–1616 / Aged 52 / This likeness taken 1603 / Age at the time 39 ys.' The label, however, appears to have been written, and presumably attached to the painting's reverse, at a later date (*circa* 1627–67, according to recent analysis).

The date given for Shakespeare's birth is suspicious, since 23 April – St George's Day – was not adopted as Shakespeare's official birthday until the eighteenth century. A whole strip of panel has disappeared from the right of the surviving portrait, and it is theoretically possible that details of the sitter's identity and age were inscribed on that part. There is a more sinister possibility: that the right-hand segment was deliberately removed at an unknown date, perhaps at the time when the paper label was concocted, because it identified the sitter as someone other than Shakespeare. A further point that undermines claims made for Sanders as an image of Shakespeare on the basis of the label is that the sitter is described there as being 39 – Shakespeare's age in 1603. It is generally felt that this sitter looks a good deal younger than that.[6] Sanders appears to be an early example of a genuine portrait from Shakespeare's lifetime that may have been wrongly presented – on the paper label – as an image of him. A collection of essays on the Sanders portrait was published in 2002, but presented no conclusive argument for its authenticity.[7]

36 The Sanders portrait.

The case of the so-called 'Grafton portrait', first brought to
public notice in 1914, is rather different (FIG. 37). This, too, is
a genuine portrait belonging to Shakespeare's period, and the
subject's age corresponds with Shakespeare's: 24 in 1588. Its
immediate geographical origins, before it reached public view,
are remote from places linked with Shakespeare. It had belonged
to the Misses Ludgate of Winston, a village on the River Tees
in County Durham, but was bequeathed to the John Rylands
Library in Manchester by one Thomas Kay in 1914. Were this to
be a genuine portrait of a youthful Shakespeare, some explanation
would be needed for the object's provenance in a remote part of
the north-east, not far from the Scottish Borders. But a much
more serious difficulty makes it virtually inconceivable that this
is a portrait of Shakespeare. It is not clear where Shakespeare
was in 1588. He was probably, in the opinion of several of his
biographers, a recent recruit to one of the playing companies then
touring in the Midlands, such as Leicester's Men or the Queen's
Men. Certainly he was at a stage in his life in which he urgently
needed gainful employment, for at home in Stratford were his wife
Anne and three children under the age of 4. If Shakespeare had
either joined, or was soon about to join, a company of players in
1588, he presumably did so in the hope of making enough money
to be able to contribute substantially to the support of his young
family. It seems highly unlikely either that this was a year in
which he could have afforded to pay a professional limner for a
good portrait, or that he had already at this early date acquired
a wealthy patron willing to fund such a work.

The record of the sitter's age may be significant in terms of
his possible identity. Paint sampling has revealed that his age was
originally inscribed as '23', but was later changed to 24. For a
serious-minded youth – and this young man looks fairly solemn
– the age 24 was significant, for it was only on reaching that age

37 The Grafton portrait.

Principum   amicitias!

that a young man qualified for ordination to deacon's orders in the Church of England, with ordination to the priesthood allowable from the age of 25. This is, I suspect, a 'coming of age' portrait of a young man whose age just happens to be close to that of Shakespeare. His circumstances, however, were very different: he was a gentleman – possibly even a nobleman – in a fine slashed doublet with gold wire buttons. He has probably attended one of the universities and is perhaps now contemplating a career in the Church. The Grafton attribution has continued, but may in truth be of little relevance: 'The owners recalled an old family tradition that the portrait had been bequeathed by one of the dukes of Grafton to their ancestor, a yeoman farmer in the village of Grafton, Northamptonshire, five or six generations previously.'

Even if some sort of genuine provenance lies behind this 'old family tradition', it brings us no closer to Shakespeare. But in essence it seems improbable. It gives the painting extremely grand aristocratic connections, yet fails to explain why an eminent duke would bequeath it to 'a yeoman farmer'. As we have seen in the case of Chandos, there is a tendency for works of art to be named after the most aristocratic of their owners.

It is rather in the same spirit that a fine Jacobean portrait for which Shakespearean claims have been made as recently as 2009 is now generally alluded to as the 'Cobbe portrait' (FIG. 38). This relates to its former owner, Charles Cobbe, archbishop of Dublin (1686–1765). Claims that it is both a portrait of Shakespeare and was painted from life were made by the archbishop's descendant Alec Cobbe, a distinguished designer, painter, picture restorer and collector of historic keyboard instruments. According to a press release issued on 9 March 2009, Alec Cobbe was excited to observe the strong resemblance of the painting that now hangs in the Folger Shakespeare Library in Washington DC to this particular item in his own inherited collection of paintings. He

38 The Cobbe portrait.

D.D. Tho: Overbury Arm de Barton in Com. Warw

saw it in London while it was on loan to the National Portrait Gallery for its *Searching for Shakespeare* exhibition. The Folger portrait has at some point been inscribed with an age and date that correspond with Shakespeare's: *Aetate 46/1610* – that is, '[the subject was] of the age of 46 in 1610'. However, the inscription is suspicious, since the subject of the portrait looks both much younger than 46 and considerably more aristocratic than Shakespeare. Like the Sanders portrait discussed above, it appears to have had an inscription added to it at a date later than when it was made.

Since an investigation in 1997, experts at the Folger no longer regard their painting as a portrait of Shakespeare. This was pointed out by Erin C. Blake in a substantial letter to the *Times Literary Supplement.*[8] The Folger portrait is now seen as a handsome example of a clutch of portraits of Sir Thomas Overbury (1581–1613). One of these was bequeathed to the Bodleian Library in 1740 by a member of the Overbury family (FIG. 39). There are good reasons why – in addition to the Overbury family – several Jacobean noblemen, including Henry Wriothesley, 3rd earl of Southampton, appear to have possessed portraits of Sir Thomas Overbury. A talented and ambitious young courtier, Overbury was a close friend and ally of Sir Robert Carr, who in turn was in high favour with King James I. Shakespeare's former patron, the earl of Southampton, was also one of Overbury's political allies.

Early in 1613 Overbury unwisely overplayed his hand in objecting passionately and publicly to the forthcoming marriage of his close friend Robert Carr to Frances, née Howard. She was already married to the earl of Essex, but the union was allegedly unconsummated. Overbury's religious views tended towards Puritanism. Also, in addition to being apparently bigamous, the forthcoming nuptials posed a severe threat to Overbury's hitherto close friendship with Carr. The ambitious Overbury had already

39 Portrait of Sir Thomas Overbury, 1613. Bodleian Library, LP 74.

got himself disliked by King James's consort, Queen Anne, and his opposition to the Carr–Howard marriage earned him the deep disfavour of the king also. Overbury's arrest (probably by royal command), imprisonment in the Tower of London and death – apparently not from natural causes – only four months later were brought to full public notice as a fascinating scandal by the murder trial that later ensued.

This was arguably the most sensational affair of the whole of James's 25-year reign. It was hugely divisive. Courtiers and noblemen who had been Overbury's friends and political allies were likely to have wished for visual mementoes of this promising young courtier who had possibly been poisoned, and possibly by royal command. Given the large number that survive, there may at one time have been several more versions of Thomas Overbury's portrait, all of them originally serving as precious mementoes of a brilliant young courtier whose life had been cut short. I suspect that they all derive from a miniature or painting done from life in 1610/11, in the period when Overbury was a rising star at court.

Supporters of the claim that the Cobbe portrait represents Shakespeare have offered various kinds of evidence, none convincing in the view of the present writer. For instance, Alec Cobbe and others have suggested that Cobbe is the master portrait from which other examples have been copied. They base this claim partly on an alleged association between this item in the Cobbe collection and Henry Wriothesley, 3rd earl of Southampton and Shakespeare's earliest known patron. However, attempts to find evidence to support this scenario have proved both circumstantial and unsound, as quietly but devastatingly argued by Robert Bearman.[9]

There are points to add about the image itself that specifically concern the Cobbe portrait, not the various kindred versions. It bears aloft, in rather large gilt letters, the words *Principum amicitias!*

– 'The alliances of princes!' A strained circumstantial argument has been put forward for this. It has been suggested that the fact that this two-word motto, from Horace's *Odes* 2.1, occurs in a poem addressed to a man who was, among much else, a playwright, somehow points towards Shakespeare. This is surely neither here nor there. The words have a clear and immediate application to the grim tale of Sir Thomas Overbury's life at court, and his ensuing gruesome death. Overbury's energy and promise were brought to nothing as a direct consequence of 'the alliances of princes' – in this case the Carr–Howard marriage, enthusiastically blessed by both the king and the queen, two potent princes. Their support for the alliance between Robert Carr and Frances Howard was to lead to Overbury's death. Another point has not been previously discussed. Not only is the two-word inscription on the Cobbe portrait painted in larger letters than one normally encounters in a mid-Jacobean portrait, and unusually located across the top of the painting, but it ends with an exclamation mark. Marks (or points) of exclamation were rarely used in this way during Shakespeare's lifetime. I for one have never seen another example of the appearance of an exclamation mark on a Jacobean portrait.

According to Overbury's biographer John Considine, there were two periods in which Overbury, and portraits of him, are likely to have been of particular interest: 'the years 1615–16, and the early 1650s'. The first period is that of the murder trials that followed Overbury's death, while the second was 'just after the execution of Charles I'.[10] Just conceivably, the Cobbe portrait may have been painted within Shakespeare's lifetime – after the death of Thomas Overbury, but a couple of years before the death of Shakespeare. The motto, however, appears to me to be a late addition that served to emphasize, for the edification of later generations, the grave dangers that could be incurred by objecting to an alliance favoured by a monarch. It is also possible that this is a much later copy of Overbury's portrait, belonging to the 1650s, in which Horace's *Ode*, which concerns civil disturbances and the causes of war, might seem especially relevant.

It is unfortunate, in the view of the present writer, that the identification of the Cobbe image as a lifetime portrait of Shakespeare was so eagerly embraced by Professor Stanley Wells and others associated with Stratford-upon-Avon, including the town's tourist board. The image is to be seen everywhere in Stratford, and is much used as a selling point in the RSC's gift shop. I believe that a nearby pub now uses it as an inn sign. It is a handsome painting, and especially so after its most recent restoration. But I, for one, am not persuaded that it has any connection with Shakespeare, beyond possibly belonging to the early Jacobean period.

The Chandos portrait, discussed in the previous chapter, continues to hold its own. Not only is it the painted image of Shakespeare that has the best claim to authenticity, having been apparently created by a young man well known to Shakespeare, and almost certainly done from life; it also appears attractively expressive. It shows its subject in a relaxed mood, wearing the casual clothes traditionally donned by players offstage. His lips are very slightly parted, as if he is just about to speak. While the great body of Shakespeare's writings bears witness to his versatility in articulating the passions and aspirations of a huge array of characters, this painting, uniquely, hints at Shakespeare's own voice and presence.

Notes

PROLOGUE

1. Quoted by Charlotte Higgins in her article 'To Find the Mind's Construction in the Face: The Great Shakespeare Debate', *Guardian*, 11 March 2009.

CHAPTER I

1. From a leader in the *Guardian* by Roy Hattersley, quoted by Katherine Duncan-Jones in her review article 'Fame in a Feigned Oval', *Times Literary Supplement*, 17 March 2006.
2. James R. Boaden, *An Inquiry into the Authenticity of Various Pictures and Prints which have been Offered to the Public as Portraits of Shakespeare* (London 1824).
3. *The Three Parnassus Plays* (1598–1601), ed. J.B. Leishman (London 1949), 185.
4. A unique manuscript text, which may come from one of the play's original actors and/or audience members – possibly Edmund Rishton, whose name appears on the flyleaf. Bodleian MS Rawl. B. 398.
5. David Piper, *The Image of the Poet: British Poets and Their Portraits* (Oxford 1982), 20.
6. For a much fuller account, see Margaret Bullard, 'Talking Heads: The Bodleian Frieze, its Inspiration, Sources, Design and Significance', *Bodleian Library Record*, 14.6 (April 1994), 461–500. Because of severe decay and damage, this frieze has undergone several major restorations which were in effect virtually new work, one in 1714, another in 1795, and yet another, most recently, in 1954.
7. W.H. Clennell, 'Bodley, Sir Thomas (1545–1613), Scholar, Diplomat, and Founder of the Bodleian Library', *Oxford Dictionary of National Biography*.
8. Bodleian MS Arch. G d.41.
9. See Katherine Duncan-Jones, *Shakespeare: Upstart Crow to Sweet Swan* (London 2011), 97–8.
10. Bodleian MS Arch. G d.47.

11. See Bernard H. Newdigate, *Michael Drayton and his Circle* (Oxford 1961), frontispiece and 212, 214, 217.

12. See Adam White, 'Love, Loyalty and Friendship: Lady Anne Clifford's Church Monuments', in Karen Hearn and Lynn Hulse, eds, *Lady Anne Clifford*, Yorkshire Archaeological Society Paper No. 7 (Leeds 2009), 54–5.

13. See *Cambridge Edition of the Works of Ben Jonson*, general eds D. Bevington, M. Butler and Ian Donaldson (Cambridge 2012), vol. 5, 170, 171–2. For a more detailed account of Ben Jonson's portraiture, see Hearn and Hulse, eds, *Lady Anne Clifford*.

14. Ian Donaldson, *Ben Jonson: A Life* (Oxford 2011), 350–56.

CHAPTER 2

1. Brian Kemp, *English Church Monuments* (London 1980), 75.

2. Kemp, *Church Monuments*, 77.

3. I refer to this distinguished family of sculptors of Flemish origin as Johnson rather than Janssen, or any other of the various spellings of the surname. The individual who was supposedly the chief craftsman in charge of this commission was Gerard; however, it is likely that his son Nicholas was in charge. For a fuller account of this family, see Adam White, 'Johnson (formerly Janssen) Family (1570–1630), Sculptors', *Oxford Dictionary of National Biography*.

4. Katherine Duncan-Jones, *Shakespeare: An Ungentle Life* (London 2010), 111.

5. Nigel Llewellyn, *Funeral Monuments in Post-Reformation England* (Cambridge 2000), 69, 181.

6. Ibid., 186.

7. Mary Edmond, 'Heminges, John (bap. 1566, d. 1630), Editor of Shakespeare's First Folio', *Oxford Dictionary of National Biography*.

8. i.e. Burbage, Heminges and Condell.

9 John Dover Wilson, *The Essential Shakespeare: A Biographical Adventure* (Cambridge 1932), 5.

10. M.H. Spielmann, 'Shakespeare's Portraiture', in *Studies in the First Folio Written for the Shakespeare Association* (Oxford 1924), 1–52.

11. See Richard T. Godfrey, *Wenceslaus Hollar: A Bohemian Artist in England* (New Haven and London 1994), 12.

12. Spielmann, 'Portraiture', 20–3.

13. Samuel Schoenbaum, *Shakespeare's Lives* (Oxford 1970), 187.

14. Ibid.

15. Ibid., 24.

16. Kemp, *Church Monuments*, 82, 85.

17. *Passenger*: passer-by.

18. Envious: malicious, spiteful.

19. I.e. 'died'.

20. This should read 'SITH', and is evidently a mistake by the carver that he was not able to correct.

21. Translated as: 'He died in the year of Our Lord 1616, at the age of 53, on 23 April.'

22. Sidney Lee, rev. Elizabeth Haresnape, 'Digges. Leonard (1588–1635), Poet and Translator', *Oxford Dictionary of National Biography*.

23. See Katherine Duncan-Jones, 'Afterword: Stow's Remains', in Ian Gadd and Alexandra Gillespie, eds, *John Stow (1525–1605) and the Making of the English Past* (London 2004), 157–63.

24. Llewellyn, *Funeral Monuments*, 108.

25. See Hugh Trevor Roper, 'Sutton, Thomas (1532–1611)', *Oxford Dictionary of National Biography*.

26. See A.J. Loomie, 'Manners, Francis, Sixth Earl of Rutland (1578–1632), Nobleman', *Oxford Dictionary of National Biography*; also *Searching for Shakespeare* (London 2009), 134.

27. Historical Manuscripts Commission, *Manuscripts of the Duke of Rutland* (1905), iv. 494.

28. Ibid., iv. 508.

29. Ibid., iv, 517.

30. Nikolaus Pevsner, *Leicestershire and Rutland*, rev. Elizabeth Williamson (London 1998), 106–7.

CHAPTER 3

1. For a fuller account, see Katherine Duncan-Jones, *Shakespeare: An Ungentle Life* (London 2010), 288–92.

2. M.H. Spielman, 'Shakespeare's Portraiture', in *Studies in the First Folio Written for the Shakespeare Association* (Oxford 1924), 32.

3. For a discussion of the ruff and doublet shown in Droeshout, see Tarnya Cooper et al., *Searching for Shakespeare* (London 2006), 48–50.

4. See Anthony James West, *The Shakespeare First Folio: The History of the Book* (Oxford 2001), 5–6.

5. Spielmann, 'Shakespeare's Portraiture', 25.

6. Mary Edmond, '"It was for Gentle Shakespeare Cut"', *Shakespeare Quarterly*, 42.3 (Autumn 1991); see also Edward Town, 'A Biographical Dictionary of London Painters 1547–1625', *Walpole Society* 76 (2014), 75.

7. *sc.*: *sculpsit*; that is, engraved (the portrait).

8. Spielmann, 'Shakespeare's Portraiture', 42.

9. Cooper et al., *Searching for Shakespeare*, 72–5.

10. Ibid., 72.

CHAPTER 4

This chapter is closely based on Katherine Duncan-Jones, 'A precious memento: The Chandos Portrait and Shakespeare's "intimate Friend"', *Times Literary Supplement*, 25 April 2014.

1. See Tarnya Cooper, *Searching for Shakespeare* (London 2006), 53–6.
2. Michael Caines, *Shakespeare and the Eighteenth Century* (Oxford 2013), 27–31.
3. See Andrew Gurr, 'Taylor, Joseph (bap. 1586, d. 1652), Actor', *Oxford Dictionary of National Biography*.

CHAPTER 5

1. Marcia Pointon in Tarnya Cooper et al., *Searching for Shakespeare* (London 2006), 221.
2. Michael Dobson, *The Making of the National Poet* (Oxford 1992), 135–6.
3. Ibid., 135–6.
4. Ibid., 146.
5. Ibid., 165.
6. See Cooper et al., *Searching for Shakespeare*, 66.
7. Stephanie Nolen, ed., *Shakespeare's Face* (Toronto 2002).
8. Erin C. Blake, 'Not a Shakespeare Portrait', *Times Literary Supplement*, 17 April 2009.
9. Robert Bearman, review of a book by Stanley Wells, *Shakespeare Found! A Life Portrait at Last* (2011), published by the Shakespeare Birthplace Trust, in *Shakespeare Quarterly*, 62.2 (Summer 2011), 281–4.
10. John Considine, 'Overbury, Sir Thomas (bap. 1581, d. 1613), courtier and author', *Oxford Dictionary of National Biography*.

Bibliography

BOOKS AND ARTICLES

Bearman, Robert, review of Stanley Wells, *Shakespeare Found! A Life Portrait at Last*, Shakespeare Birthplace Trust (Stratford-upon-Avon 2009), *Shakespeare Quarterly*, 62.2 (Summer 2011).

Bevington, D., Martin Butler and Ian Donaldson, eds, *Cambridge Edition of the Works of Ben Jonson* (Oxford 1961).

Boaden, James R., *An Inquiry into the Authenticity of Various Pictures and Prints which have been Offered to the Public as Portraits of Shakespeare* (London 1824).

Bullard, Margaret, R.A., 'Talking Heads: The Bodleian Frieze, its Inspiration, Sources, Design and Significance', *Bodleian Library Record*, 14.6 (April 1994).

Caines, Michael, *Shakespeare and the Eighteenth Century* (Oxford 2013).

Clennell, W.H., 'Bodley, Sir Thomas (1545–1613), Scholar, Diplomat, and Founder of the Bodleian Library', *Oxford Dictionary of National Biography*.

Considine, John, 'Overbury, Thomas (bap. 1581, d. 1613), Courtier and Author)', *Oxford Dictionary of National Biography*.

Cooper, Tarnya, et al., *Searching for Shakespeare* (London 2006).

Dobson, Michael, *The Making of the National Poet* (Oxford 1992).

Donaldson, Ian, *Ben Jonson: A Life* (Oxford 2011).

Duncan-Jones, Katherine, 'Afterword: Stow's Remains', in Ian Gadd and Alexandra Gillespie, eds, *John Stow (1525–1605) and the Making of the English Past* (London 2004), 157–63.

Duncan-Jones, Katherine, 'Fame in a Feigned Oval', *Times Literary Supplement*, 17 March 2006.

Duncan-Jones, Katherine, *Shakespeare: An Ungentle Life* (London 2010).

Duncan-Jones, Katherine, *Shakespeare: Upstart Crow to Sweet Swan* (London 2011).

Edmond, Mary, 'Heminges, John (bap. 1566, d. 1630), Editor of Shakespeare's First Folio', *Oxford Dictionary of National Biography*.

Edmond, Mary, ' "It was for Gentle Shakespeare Cut"', *Shakespeare Quarterly*, 42.3 (Autumn 1991), 339–44.

Godfrey, Richard T., *Wenceslaus Hollar: A Bohemian Artist in England* (New Haven CT and London 1924).

Gurr, Andrew, 'Taylor, Joseph (bap. 1586, d.1652), Actor', *Oxford Dictionary of National Biography*.

Higgins, Charlotte, 'To Find the Mind's Construction in the Face: The Great Shakespeare Debate', *Guardian*, 11 March 2009.

Historical Manuscripts Commission, *Manuscripts of the Duke of Rutland* (London 1905), iv. 494.

Kemp, Brian, *English Church Monuments* (London 1980).

Lee, Sidney, revised by Elizabeth Haresnape, 'Digges, Leonard (1588–1635), Poet and Translator', *Oxford Dictionary of National Biography*.

Leishman, J.B., ed., *The Three Parnassus Plays (1598–1601)* (London 1949).

Llewellyn, Nigel, *Funeral Monuments in Post-Reformation England* (Cambridge 2000).

Loomie, A.J., 'Manners, Francis, Sixth Earl of Rutland (1578–1632) , nobleman', *Oxford Dictionary of National Biography*.

Maguire, Laurie, and Emma Smith, *30 Great Myths about Shakespeare* (Oxford 2012).

Newdigate, Bernard H., *Michael Drayton and his Circle* (Oxford 1961).

Nolen, Stephanie, ed., *Shakespeare's Face* (Toronto 2002) rev. Elizabeth Williamson (London 1998).

Piper, David, *The Image of the Poet: British Poets and their Portraits* (Oxford 1982).

Schoenbaum, Samuel, *Shakespeare's Lives* (Oxford 1970).

Spielmann, M.H., 'Shakespeare's Portraiture', in *Studies in the First Folio Written for the Shakespeare Association* (Oxford 1924).

Town, Edward, 'A Biographical Dictionary of London Painters 1547–1625', *Walpole Society*, 76 (2014), 1–253.

Trevor Roper, Hugh, 'Sutton, Thomas (1532–1611)', *Oxford Dictionary of National Biography*.

West, Anthony James, *The Shakespeare First Folio: The History of the Book* (Oxford 2001).

White, Adam, 'Johnson (formerly Janssen) Family (1570–1630), Sculptors', *Oxford Dictionary of National Biography*.

White, Adam, 'Love, Loyalty and Friendship', in Karen Hearn and Lynn Hulse, eds, *Lady Anne Clifford: Culture, Patronage and Gender in Seventeenth-century Britain*, Yorkshire Archaeological Society Paper No. 7 (Leeds 2009).

Wilson, John Dover, *The Essential Shakespeare: A Biographical Adventure* (Cambridge 1932).

MANUSCRIPTS

Bodleian MS. Rawl. B. 398 (text of *The First Part of the Return from Parnassus*).

Bodleian MS. Arch. Gd.41 (Edmond Malone's inscribed copy of the first edition of *Shakespeare's Sonnets* (1609)).

British Library MS. Add. 21,111 (George Vertue notebook).

Image sources

Acknowledgements

I have received generous help and support from the following: Dr Tarnya Cooper, Professor Brian Kemp, Professor Nigel Llewellyn, Professor Laurie Maguire, Dr Emma Smith, David Vaisey and Dr Jacqueline Watson. I am also grateful to the ever helpful staff of the Bodleian Library, especially those who work in the Upper Reading Room. At a late stage this book has also benefited from the highly skilled scrutiny of Janet Phillips and Lucy Morton.

Index

References to illustrations are in *red*